LIVING THE WAY OF JESUS

Practicing the Christian Calendar One Week at a Time

MICHAELE LAVIGNE

To Austin and Galilee
May you discover the great joy of living the way of Jesus!

Copyright © 2019 by Michaele LaVigne
The Foundry Publishing
PO Box 419527
Kansas City, MO 64141
thefoundrypublishing.com

978-0-8341-3836-0

Printed in the
United States of America

All rights reserved. No part of this publication may be reproduced, stored in a retrieval system, or transmitted in any form or by any means—for example, electronic, photocopy, recording—without the prior written permission of the publisher. The only exception is brief quotations in printed reviews.

Cover Design: J.R. Caines
Interior Design: Mike Williams

Library of Congress Cataloging-in-Publication Data
A complete catalog record for this book is available from the Library of Congress.

All Scripture quotations, unless indicated, are taken from The Holy Bible: New International Version® (NIV®). Copyright © 1973, 1978, 1984, 2011 by Biblica, Inc. Used by permission of Zondervan. All rights reserved worldwide. www.zondervan.com.

Scripture quotations marked NLT are taken from the Holy Bible, New Living Translation, copyright © 1996, 2004, 2015 by Tyndale House Foundation. Used by permission of Tyndale House Publishers, Inc., Carol Stream, Illinois 60188. All rights reserved.

Scripture quotations marked MSG are taken from THE MESSAGE, copyright © 1993, 2002, 2018 by Eugene H. Peterson. Used by permission of NavPress. All rights reserved. Represented by Tyndale House Publishers, Inc.

The internet addresses, email addresses, and phone numbers in this book are accurate at the time of publication. They are provided as a resource. The Foundry Publishing does not endorse them or vouch for their content or permanence.

10 9 8 7 6 5 4 3 2 1

CONTENTS

Practicing Gratitude — 5
Introduction — 7

Year A

The Season of Advent — 10
The Twelve Days of Christmas — 15
The Season of Epiphany — 18
The Season of Lent — 28
The Season of Easter — 35
Holy Days: Ascension, Pentecost, Trinity Sunday — 42
Ordinary Time — 47
Practices for Not-so-Ordinary Time: Vacation, Elections, Tragedy — 75
Christ the King Sunday — 79

Year B

The Season of Advent — 82
The Twelve Days of Christmas — 87
The Season of Epiphany — 90
The Season of Lent — 100
The Season of Easter — 107
Holy Days: Ascension, Pentecost, Trinity Sunday — 114
Ordinary Time — 119
Practices for Not-so-Ordinary Time: Vacation, Elections, Tragedy — 147
Christ the King Sunday — 151

Year C

The Season of Advent	154
The Twelve Days of Christmas	159
The Season of Epiphany	162
The Season of Lent	172
The Season of Easter	179
Holy Days: Ascension, Pentecost, Trinity Sunday	186
Ordinary Time	191
Practices for Not-so-Ordinary Time: Vacation, Elections, Tragedy	219
Christ the King Sunday	223

PRACTICING GRATITUDE

When I think about all that has happened to put this book into your hands, there is so much for which I am grateful. Here is my own, though not exhaustive, list of gratitude.

I am grateful for the faithfulness of many, many people who have fostered me in the way of Jesus: My parents, Doug and Debbie, were my first introduction to Jesus, and their lives of obedience and love have taught me more than any others what living the way of Jesus is all about. My beloved brothers, Ben, Caleb, and Josh, have provided me with thirty-four years' worth of practices in humility, making amends, receiving love, and much laughter. The Boquist and Flemming families into which I was born, and the Shuck and LaVigne families into which I married all contain generations of women and men who have lived the way of Jesus. I am keenly aware that I am walking this way only because of so many who have gone before and have shared with me about it.

I am grateful for the many gifts of the 8th Street Church. Being their pastor is my great joy, and has been the second-greatest spiritually formative experience of my life. I am grateful for the humility, the shared desire for transformation, and the commitment to being good neighbors that are embodied by this people. I am grateful for people young and old who are willing to practice the way of Jesus and who therefore provided the opportunity for me to write the practices here. I am grateful for the stories of hope and transformation we have shared together as we've practiced the way of Jesus.

I am grateful for the people who have directly contributed to this endeavor: my friend and teammate Chris Pollock, whose holy imagination continually sparks my own, as evidenced by these practices, which almost all began in our Thursday morning conversations as we planned for Sunday; my dear friend Janie Kirt Morris, who, during the course of this project, provided ample encouragement and occasional food; Banning Dawson, whose advice and liturgical wisdom helped shape this book and whose words of affirmation kept me going; Jessica McDaniel, who painstakingly combed through my many words and misplaced commas.

I am grateful for the cloud of witnesses in the here and now: friends who have encouraged me to write—Tara Beth, Carlee, Tara, Hope, Nick, Kathleen, Tiffany, and Sunie; Nancy, my spiritual director, who has been a faithful presence throughout many years; Holly, Claudine, and Andrea, my sisters-in-arms who have seen this process from the beginning and have seen me through my best and worst.

I am so very grateful for the three most wonderful gifts of my family: Austin and Galilee, who have no idea what I've been writing or why I've spent long nights at the office but who remind me every day why I want to practice living the way of Jesus. Being their mother is the greatest spiritually formative experience of my life. They are often my greatest teachers, and I pray God helps me become theirs. And Brent—my best friend, my partner, my husband—who has not only walked with me in the late nights and overwhelmed moments of ministry but has also encouraged me to be the best Michaele I can be, for more than twenty years. As our Swazi friends say, "My mouth does not have enough tongues to say thank you enough." I am full of gratitude for him and for the very good God who gave us to each other.

Finally, I am so filled with gratitude for Jesus, who has offered himself to me not only as Lord and King but also as my Friend who knows the way and who guides me in it every day. Blessing and honor, glory and power be unto him!

INTRODUCTION

Each week, I say these words to our congregation, following the sermon and Communion of our worship: "We are invited not only to *hear* the way of Jesus once a week but also to *live* the way of Jesus every day. So you are invited to take a practice with you into the week, that we might live this way of Jesus together." I then explain the weekly practice printed in our worship folders, which is written in conjunction with that week's sermon.

In our short life together (our church was planted in 2015), we have taken on practices like driving the speed limit, having an honest conversation about failure, finding new ways to pray, meeting someone from a different culture, and figuring out how to practice real Sabbath. These weekly practices have become part of the fabric of our lives together as we've developed a beautiful habit of *doing* things with what we've heard. And, though I may be a bit biased, I can say that the people of the 8th Street Church have become the most hospitable, generous, courageous, and healing congregation I've ever seen.

Looking back, it is evident to see what I only guessed at in the beginning: we needed to *practice* our way into becoming who we wanted to be. Slowly but surely, after we've been practicing for a while, we realize we can do things we couldn't do before. Yet, while we practice this Jesus way, we certainly do not control our own growth or transformation. We are not practicing to fulfill our own desires or to gain greater control of our lives. In fact, the practices we take on have the opposite effect: we practice our way into *dependence*, not independence. This idea is certainly not new with me. John Wesley, the eighteenth-century pastor, evangelist, and founder of Methodism, invited communities into very specific practices to experience transformation together. So maybe we don't need new things; maybe we just need to remember the old things, and reimagine them in our context today.

HOW TO USE THIS BOOK

This book is organized around the Christian calendar, using Revised Common Lectionary texts for most weeks. The Revised Common Lectionary—or, hereafter, simply the Lectionary—is a compilation of scriptural texts that follows the seasons of the Christian calendar over a three-year cycle. The practices in this book follow the same pattern. If you are new to the Christian calendar, I invite you to walk through this ancient way of keeping time as part of living the way of Jesus. The rhythms of the Christian calendar orient us to God's reality. We do not merely ask God to join our lives; instead, we are invited to participate in *God's* life. Subtly and explicitly, this way of marking time reminds us that we are part of a story that is different from the stories we hear all around us. Practices specific to each season enable us to engage further with this larger story and help us in the process of reorientation to this different way of keeping time.

SOME WORDS FOR PASTORS

During the formal seasons of the church calendar, each practice is connected to one of the Lectionary texts for that Sunday. Pastors who already preach from the Lectionary may want to use or adapt the weekly practice as our congregation has—as a way to live out the message of the sermon. But even if you don't follow the Lectionary, my hope is that these practices give you resources and spark your own creativity as you invite your congregation to live the way of Jesus. You will also notice that each practice has a place to notate when that practice was used, to help you map out your congregation's journey.

SOME WORDS FOR INDIVIDUALS AND GROUPS

This book is not meant to be a Bible study or daily devotional. Instead, it is best suited to complement your regular pattern of reading and Bible study, and to provide a way to practice what you read and learn. If you are beginning this journey as an individual, I invite you to consider at least one other person to walk through these practices with. Living the way of Jesus is never a solo enterprise!

If you already have a group of people gathered for small group or Bible study, this material would be a wonderful guide for your life together. Each time you gather, decide what practice you will take on together the next week, whether you follow the Lectionary outline or choose your own pattern. Your discussion each week can revolve around the question posed at the end of each practice: What did I learn about myself and/or God in this practice?

Whoever you are, and however you choose to use the practices here, I offer these words of benediction as you begin: *May you know the joy, peace, and transforming power of God as you live the way of Jesus!*

YEAR A

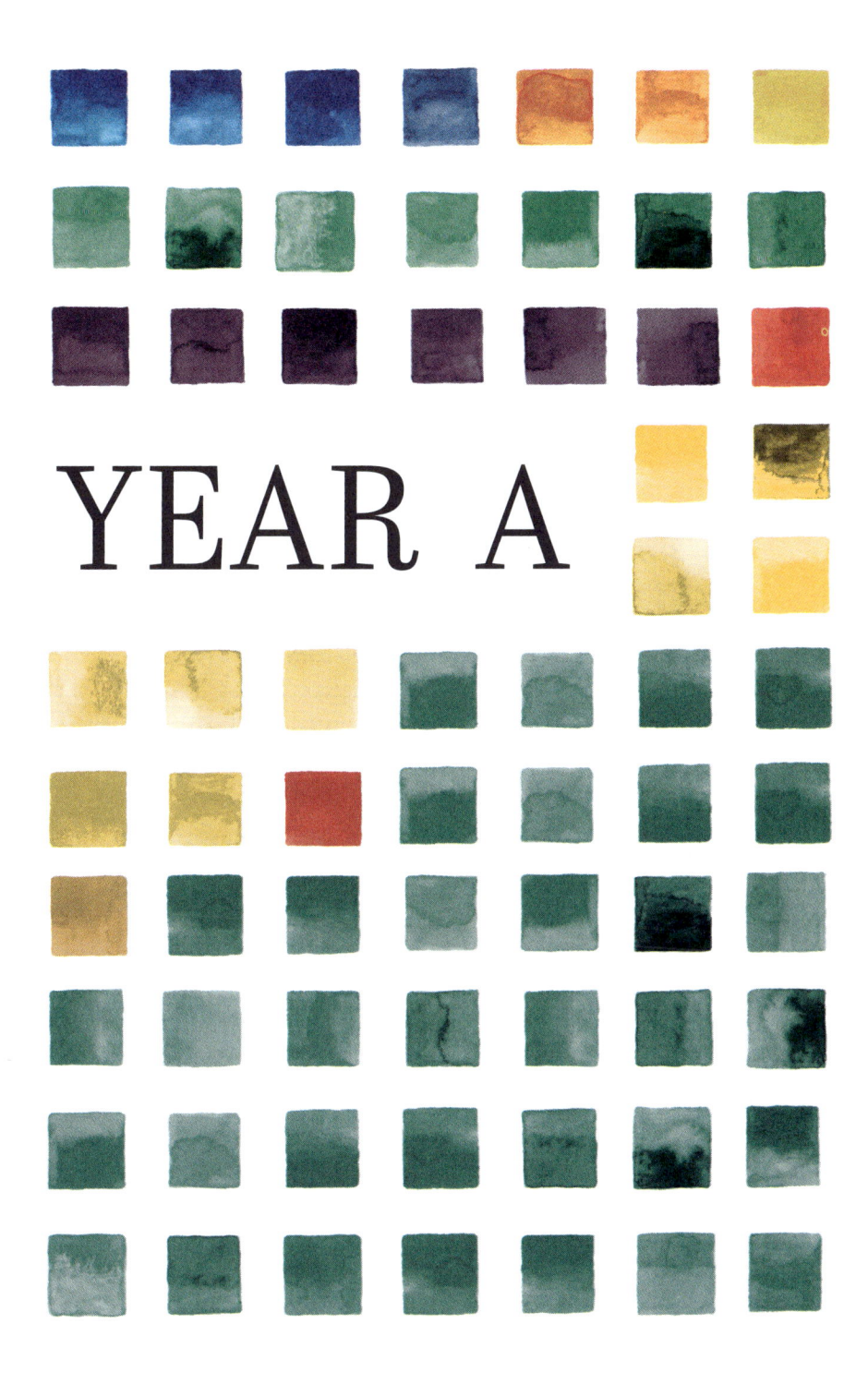

THE SEASON OF ADVENT

We often assume Advent is the countdown to Christmas: the church equivalent of how many shopping days we have left. The season does begin four Sundays prior to Christmas Day, but we aren't preparing ourselves for Christ coming as a baby. Instead, Advent is the preparation of people who live in the in-between: looking back on Christ's birth, and looking forward to when Christ will come again.

As a result, the scriptures of Advent feel decidedly un-Christmasy. They are filled with prophetic words of judgment against oppressive earthly powers and proclamations of the justice and peace that will replace these powers in God's kingdom. Advent is not so much a season of light and hope as a season of waiting in the dark.

It is significant that the Christian calendar begins this way. We begin the year in an honest place, admitting that we do, in fact, need saving, and that the One who saves chooses to do it in a different way than we expect.

In these weeks, we do not celebrate the God who comes to us on *our* schedule, conforming to *our* list of requirements. In Advent, we recognize that God comes to us not in the way or timeline we *expect* but in the way we *need*. The best things—forming new life, making people whole, restoring the world—cannot be rushed.

During this season, we will take on practices that help us prepare our hearts and minds for this God who comes to us. *May we grow in awareness, trust, and expectation of our God as we wait in the dark.*

First Sunday of Advent
Be a Gossip Buster

Scripture: Isaiah 2:1-5

THE WEAPONS WE most often use against each other in daily life tend to be words rather than swords. This week, practice turning your swords into plowshares by avoiding gossip. Whenever you or someone you are with begins to speak ill of someone else or spread rumors, quickly end it. Guide the conversation to a different subject. If you're not sure whether something qualifies as gossip, imagine the subject of the conversation standing with you. If you wouldn't be having the conversation in front of that person, you probably don't need to be having it in their absence. When you hear others using words to do harm toward someone, see how quickly you can offer words to bring peace.

Date(s) Used:_____

What did I learn about myself and/or God in this practice?

Second Sunday of Advent
Provide Safety

Scripture: Isaiah 11:1-10

ISAIAH TELLS US that in God's future there is safety for all—wolves and lambs alike. The church is where this reality can be experienced even now. You can practice being a person of safety for those you encounter this week by keeping these things in mind:

- Listen well when someone is speaking; do not interrupt.
- Keep your opinions to a minimum; share only when you are asked.
- Protect the safety of those who are being mistreated by speaking up on their behalf and/or reporting the mistreatment.

Date(s) Used:_____

What did I learn about myself and/or God in this practice?

Third Sunday of Advent
Reduce, Reuse, Recycle

Scripture: Isaiah 35:1-10

THOSE WHO LIVE in wealthy areas of the world often do not see the damage created by our trash, but how humans use and discard material goods greatly affects the rest of creation. This week, join in God's care for creation by thinking carefully about what gets thrown away. Use some of these ideas to help you:

- Generate as little trash as possible, opting for non-disposable items wherever and whenever you can.
- Reduce the amount of water, disposable products, and goods you use, consuming only what is absolutely necessary.
- Reuse all materials (grocery bags, paper, containers) as much as possible before throwing them out.
- Recycle everything you can: paper, plastic, glass, and metal. If your area waste removal doesn't include recycling pickup, look online to find the nearest recycling center.

Date(s) Used:_____

What did I learn about myself and/or God in this practice?

Fourth Sunday of Advent
Naming our Fears

Scripture: Isaiah 7:10-16

FEAR IS A powerful yet subtle force that often directs our decisions and actions, as it did for King Ahaz. It may be even more powerful when we are not aware of its influence. This week, carve out at least thirty minutes for this exercise of naming your fears and allowing our with-us God—Immanuel—to release you from them.

- First, spend a few minutes calming your mind and heart. Settle in and get comfortable in silence. Invite the Holy Spirit to guide you.
- Imagine Jesus, our with-us God, asking you, "What do you fear?" Examine your heart, mind, and emotions. Write down the fears that come to you (e.g., sickness, shame, bankruptcy, loneliness, etc.).
- Look over what you have written. Imagine God being fully present to you in every circumstance listed. How does this awareness change your fears?
- Jesus who is with us offers freedom from the oppression of fear. What, if anything, would you do differently if you weren't afraid of the things on your list?
- Respond with obedience to anything the Spirit is guiding you to do, say, or write. Close your prayer with gratitude.

Date(s) Used:_____

What did I learn about myself and/or God in this practice?

THE TWELVE DAYS OF CHRISTMAS

For most American Evangelical Christians, what we know of the twelve days of Christmas is from a song—of which the only words we all know for sure are "FIVE GOLDEN RINGS!" But for most of the history of the church, Christmas has been celebrated for twelve full days, from December 25 through January 5. This short season ends with the commemoration of the Epiphany of the Magi on January 6, which ushers in the much longer season of Epiphany.

During the twelve days of Christmas, we take time to appreciate the wonder of the incarnation: God who comes to dwell with us, becoming like us. It is a season decidedly opposed to the consumer mentality that engulfs a typical American Christmas celebration. Christ is not just one of the gifts we unwrap in a hurry and forget about a few days later. These days give us time to savor, enjoy, and bask in the goodness that is God-with-us.

Christmas Day and Epiphany are always the same dates: December 25 and January 6. Because these dates fall on different days of the week each year, there may not always be two Sundays within the twelve days of Christmas. The Sunday on or immediately following January 6 is celebrated as Epiphany Sunday.

May these days of Christmas be full of joy as we receive the God who comes to us.

Christmas Day or First Sunday after Christmas
Five Details

Scripture: Luke 2:1-20

THE WONDER OF God's presence and salvation is lost on us when we forget to pay attention—even at Christmas. We are easily bored and quick to fill the time with distractions. This week, push back on hurry and distraction by practicing attentiveness. Whenever you want to distract yourself with time-eaters like social media or games, first take time to notice at least five details around you. Be attentive to things like your breath, sunlight, the taste of food, laughter, textures of carpet and curtains, the shape of a loved one's smile. Pray that this simple act of attentiveness will train your heart to be present and aware of God's activity in you and in your world.

Date(s) Used: _____

What did I learn about myself and/or God in this practice?

_____
_____
_____
_____
_____
_____

Second Sunday of Christmas or Epiphany Sunday
Prayer of Surrender

Scripture: Matthew 2:1-12

THE MAGI PUT their lives on hold and traveled for months—if not years—to worship a King who was not their own. Their actions demonstrate great humility, holy desire, and lives surrendered to God's work in the world. This week, we will look to them as models for discipleship as we pray words of surrender written by John Wesley as a part of his Covenant Service. You may want to rewrite these words and post them in a prominent place where you will see it often throughout the week. Use it as a guide to prayer every time you see it. If you do not feel you are ready to pray these words, be honest with God and with yourself. You can add to the prayer if needed: "God, I *want* to want this, but I don't. Please shape your desires within me."

> *Lord, make me what you will. I put myself fully into your hands: put me to doing, put me to suffering; let me be employed for you, or laid aside for you; let me be full, let me be empty; let me have all things, let me have nothing. I freely and with a willing heart give it all to your pleasure and disposal.*

Date(s) Used: _____

What did I learn about myself and/or God in this practice?

_____
_____
_____
_____
_____
_____

THE SEASON OF EPIPHANY

Epiphany may be the season least familiar to those of us in Protestant-Evangelical traditions. Yet it might be the most wonderful season of them all, filled with light, and joy, and pure astonishment at the wonder of God.

An epiphany is defined as "an appearance or manifestation, especially of a divine being," which is an apt description of what happened when Magi from the East discovered a star that told of a newborn king. But the story of the Magi is not just about their epiphany; it's an epiphany for us too. It reminds us that God is in the business of telling people about himself, even—and maybe especially—the people we assume don't know the first thing about God. During this season we revel in the light that God shines so that any and all can see God's glory. And, like the Magi, as we encounter the dazzling beauty of this God of light, love, and power, we find that we are changed.

Epiphany begins at the same time every year but has varying lengths depending on the date of Easter. The final Sunday in Epiphany is Transfiguration Sunday. Ash Wednesday, which marks the beginning of the season of Lent, falls in the week after Transfiguration Sunday. The date of Ash Wednesday is determined by counting back six weeks from the date of Easter. For each Lectionary year (Year A, Year B, Year C), this book includes the maximum amount of potential weeks for an Epiphany season, but most years will have fewer. Transfiguration Sunday will always be the Sunday directly preceding Ash Wednesday.

During Epiphany, we will engage in practices to help us receive the light God gives us. *May we be astonished and overjoyed—both by God's dazzling light and by what God's light grows in us.*

First Sunday after the Epiphany/ Baptism of the Lord
Waking Up Beloved

Scripture: Matthew 3:13-17

EVERY MORNING THIS week, pull your mind into wakefulness by thinking of God's love for and approval of you. Spend a few moments soaking in your grace-given identity before you have opportunity to do anything else. Just as Jesus heard his Father's words of affirmation before he performed a single miracle, allow God to remind you this week that you are loved before you tackle your to-do list, or even brush your teeth. You may want to leave a sticky note or some kind of written reminder beside your bed to help with this practice.

Date(s) Used: _____

What did I learn about myself and/or God in this practice?

Second Sunday after the Epiphany
Daily Scripture Reading

Scripture: 1 Corinthians 1:1-9

GOD WILL CERTAINLY astonish us as long as we give him the time and space to do so. This week, spend at least five minutes each day reading Scripture. If this is a new practice for you, consider setting an alarm on your phone, watch, or computer so you can read at the same time each day. If you're not sure where to start, begin in one of the Gospels, reading the story in order. Before you begin reading, ask the Holy Spirit to reveal God to you in what you read. As you encounter God, be prepared to be astonished, and open yourself to respond.

Date(s) Used:_____

What did I learn about myself and/or God in this practice?

_____

_____

_____

_____

_____

_____

YEAR A

Third Sunday after the Epiphany
Practice Diversity

Scripture: 1 Corinthians 1:10-18

THE WORLD SAYS unity can only be achieved through sameness, but the Spirit of God invites us into unity with people who are different racially, culturally, economically, and even theologically. This week, instead of practicing sameness, practice unity in the midst of diversity. Go somewhere you don't belong: visit a church of a different denomination, use a gas station on the opposite side of town, ride the bus to work if you usually drive your car, or attend an event hosted by or for those who have different views from your own. As you do one or more of these practices, pray that the Spirit will provide you more courage than caution as you live into the unity that only God provides.

Date(s) Used:_____

What did I learn about myself and/or God in this practice?

Fourth Sunday after the Epiphany
Don't Seek Credit

YEAR A

Scripture: *1 Corinthians 1:18-31*

MOST OF US know we should practice humility; therefore, we rarely boast about our accomplishments in public. But we may find that the desire to be boastful is expressed in more subtle forms of self-promoting language and behavior. We want to make ourselves look good for others, and we often work hard to make sure we get credit when we think it is due. This week, resist the urge to remind others of your good work or good ideas. Instead, every time you feel inclined toward self-promotion, be reminded of the saving power of God, which comes to us in the form of a seemingly powerless and foolish cross. Use each opportunity you have to resist boasting to be grateful for and boast in God's good work and ideas.

Date(s) Used: _____

What did I learn about myself and/or God in this practice?

Fifth Sunday after the Epiphany
Encouragement in Frustration

Scripture: 1 Corinthians 2:1-16

> "But we have this treasure in jars of clay to show that this all-surpassing power is from God and not from us."
>
> —2 Corinthians 4:7

THIS WEEK, LET these words encourage you. You may want to write them on a card and post them somewhere you can see often. Whenever you feel frustrated about your own limitations or the misunderstandings of others, remember the wisdom of this verse. Ask the Lord to enter in his grace and pick up where you leave off.

Date(s) Used: _____

What did I learn about myself and/or God in this practice?

_____
_____
_____
_____
_____
_____
_____
_____

Sixth Sunday after the Epiphany
Admitting Fault

YEAR A

Scripture: 1 Corinthians 3:1-9

BECAUSE GOD IS perfect, we don't have to be. When we admit to God, to ourselves, and to others that we don't have it all together, we find freedom in the grace that is extended to us. Then God uses our vulnerability to build trust and respect in our relationships. Often when we mess up we are hesitant to admit it, and we tend to defend ourselves rather than apologize. This week, find freedom in admitting fault. Use this nine-word script as often as you need, and pay attention to what God does in you and in those who hear it: *"I was wrong. I am sorry. Please forgive me."*

Date(s) Used:_____

What did I learn about myself and/or God in this practice?

Seventh Sunday after the Epiphany
Bless Others

Scripture: 1 Corinthians 3:10-11

THIS WEEK, THINK of your interactions with others as adding to their buildings in progress. Look for ways to bless others as you go about your regular routines, choosing to use building materials of generosity, kindness, and grace. Ask the Spirit who needs your time, advocacy, encouragement, or gift; then make plans to give of yourself. Maybe you will be led to leave an extra-large tip for a restaurant server, visit someone who's lonely, or write an encouraging letter. Notice the work of the Spirit transforming you as you work with God to bless others.

Date(s) Used:_____

What did I learn about myself and/or God in this practice?

Eighth Sunday after the Epiphany
Look Out for Comparisons

Scripture: 1 Corinthians 4:1-13

IN THE AGE of celebrity pastors and speakers, comparing and rating Christian leaders has become commonplace—but this is exactly the kind of behavior Paul rebukes in the church of Corinth, and in us. This week, look for signs of Christians exhibiting pride in one leader at the expense of another, starting with yourself. How do you see this playing out in your own local church, your community, or on social media? Each time you are tempted to compare, or when you see others comparing and judging their leaders, invite the Holy Spirit to show you a better way. Ask the Lord to help you respect and love all brothers and sisters in Christ, including your leaders as well as those you may not know personally.

Date(s) Used:_____

What did I learn about myself and/or God in this practice?

Transfiguration Sunday
Listen to Jesus

Scripture: Matthew 17:1-9

IN THE MIDST of clamor and confusion, the disciples heard the clear command to listen to Jesus; it is the same for us. This week, set aside at least five minutes each day to listen to Jesus, either by reading a story from one of the Gospels or listening in silence. Before you begin, ask the Holy Spirit to help you, and be on your guard against distractions. If you are not accustomed to listening in silence, the first few days may be difficult. But remember that you are not reading Jesus's words to figure out a secret meaning, nor are you listening for a to-do list. You are listening to the words of Jesus, which bring life, joy, and freedom.

Date(s) Used: _____

What did I learn about myself and/or God in this practice?

_____
_____
_____
_____
_____
_____

Epiphany

THE SEASON OF LENT

On Transfiguration Sunday, the brilliance of God's revelation in Jesus turns the corner into a new kind of revelation found in the journey toward the cross. Ash Wednesday, the day we remember our humanity, begins our six-week observance of Lent. It is similar to Advent in that it is a season of preparation for what is to come. In these weeks, we walk with Jesus as he makes his way to the cross, taking on a whole new understanding of what it means to be Christ's disciples.

Most of us spend a lot of time and energy moving away from failure, and deep feeling, and fear—all of which are woven into the fabric of human existence. But in Lent we observe it, we sit with it, and we lament. It is the time we look with eyes wide open at who we really are and what the world is really like. This honest assessment drives home the reality that we need God, and it increases our desire for the things of God.

For most of its two-thousand-plus-year history, the church has observed Lent with fasting and prayer. We do not fast because it's a way to earn God's favor or get God's attention (it's neither); we fast because we want to become more aware of the things that keep us from following Jesus fully. In addition to the weekly practices suggested here, you may consider a particular item or activity from which you willingly choose to abstain throughout this season. Each Sunday in Lent is considered a "feast day," in anticipation of Easter that is to come, and the fasted items can be enjoyed on those days.

In this season of Lent, we take on practices to help us see ourselves and our world as we truly are. *And, as we do, may we also learn to see God for who God truly is: the God who loves us so much that God gives Godself away.*

First Sunday in Lent
Sleep

Scripture: Matthew 4:1-11

POWER, FAME, AND comfort are enticing ways for all of us to escape the difficulties of being human. Yet, in the desert, Jesus shows us the way to make peace with the natural limitations of being human, rather than fighting against them. Our need for sleep is one of the greatest reminders that we are human, yet it is something we often fight. Whether we battle insomnia, work late into the night, or just hate lying in silence, most of us receive far less than the sleep we need. This week, practice sleep by doing one of the following:

- Choose one day to sleep until you cannot sleep any longer. *Saturday March 19*
- Go to bed when you first feel tired at night.
- Take a nap during the day.
- Schedule yourself to sleep for eight hours each night this week.

Receive sleep as a gift from your Creator, who has made you to be human.

Date(s) Used: _____

What did I learn about myself and/or God in this practice?

Second Sunday in Lent
Serve the Undeserving

YEAR A

Scripture: John 3:1-17

MANY OF US know the words of John 3:16 but forget the words that follow: Jesus was sent not to condemn the world but that the world might be saved through him. This week, join Jesus as he reaches to love and serve the undeserving: buy lunch for an offensive coworker; bake cookies for a mean neighbor; send a card to an estranged family member; offer food and conversation to a panhandler. As you do, remember with gratitude the way Christ has invited you into a whole new life with God.

Date(s) Used: 3/17/22

What did I learn about myself and/or God in this practice?

Yesterday, I bought flowers from a woman selling them at a stoplight. It led to an interesting conversation with others in the car because of the comment "I hope she uses the money for food."

I was reminded of trusting God and knowing that he asks us to give no strings attached and with no conditions.

Third Sunday in Lent
Asking for Help

Scripture: John 4:5-42

WE HAVE A Savior who was not afraid to be vulnerable. When he needed time away, he took it. When he was lonely, he asked his friends to be with him. When he was thirsty, he asked for a drink. We can admit our vulnerability too. This week, ask others to help you. You might need to borrow something from a neighbor, ask someone to reschedule a meeting if you're too busy, or simply respond honestly if someone asks you if you need help carrying something to your car. If ever you find it difficult to ask or to admit your need for help, take that as a cue for conversation with God. Ask what you can learn about yourself and about grace.

Date(s) Used:_____

What did I learn about myself and/or God in this practice?

Fourth Sunday in Lent
Contemplation/Imaginative Prayer

Scripture: *John 9:1-41*

WE MAY NOT be able to see Jesus with our eyes, but we can see him in our imagination, our mind's eye. With the Spirit to guide us, we can enter into conversations with Jesus as Scripture prompts our imagination. Set aside at least twenty minutes for this practice so you will not be distracted or interrupted.

- First, ask the Holy Spirit to guide your imagination.
- Read all of John 9 slowly, perhaps choosing an unfamiliar version so you're not tempted to skim over familiar words. It often helps to read out loud.
- As you read, allow the words to create pictures in your mind, and ask Jesus to show himself to you.
- When you see him, pause to reflect on the image without hurrying. What expression do you see on his face? What is he doing? Who else is there?
- Ask questions as they arise, and listen for how Jesus responds.
- Write down anything you want to remember from this conversation. Reflect on the ways your eyes were opened as you talked with Jesus.

Date(s) Used:_____

What did I learn about myself and/or God in this practice?

Fifth Sunday in Lent
Write an Encouraging Note

Scripture: John 11:1-45

JESUS IS THE only one who can raise the dead to life, but he invites the whole community to witness and participate. Even though we may not be able to roll away the tombstone or untangle someone's grave clothes, there are many other ways we can join in Jesus's work. This week, take time to write a note of encouragement to someone who is sick or facing a difficult situation. Ask the Lord to lead you to the words that will partner with the Spirit's work in that person's life.

Date(s) Used:_____

What did I learn about myself and/or God in this practice?

Palm Sunday/Sixth Sunday in Lent
Entertainment Fast

Scripture: Matthew 21:1-11

OUR CULTURE IS saturated in entertainment. Thanks to streaming services and smartphones, we can dip in and out of other people's stories all day long. We use entertainment to distract ourselves from the pain, mess, or boredom of real life—and that's not inherently wrong. But we often end up distracting ourselves from the story of God that is found within the pain, mess, and boredom. This week, pull the plug on all entertainment. Instead of filling every moment with distraction, make peace with the silence. Read, remember, and ponder the events of Holy Week as you prepare for Easter. Follow Jesus's activities in this week as recorded in Matthew 21–27. Allow the Jesus story to be the only story you enter into this week, and stay there.

Date(s) Used:_____

What did I learn about myself and/or God in this practice?

THE SEASON OF EASTER

On Easter Sunday we celebrate God's promise of resurrection coming to life in the resurrected Christ—the future reality rushing into our present moment. But Easter is not something we can encapsulate in a single day. It requires a fifty-day season to probe, ponder, and practice the deep and wonderful mystery of resurrection.

The ancients referred to Easter as the eighth day of creation because, on Easter, God began the work of making all things new, beginning with resurrecting Christ from the dead. In Easter we hear God proclaim, "I am making everything new!" (Revelation 21:5), and we affirm that, indeed, "the old has gone, the new is here!" (2 Corinthians 5:17).

When we observe Easter as a season, we have time to experience that resurrection is God's new creation made real not just in Jesus but also in all of us who are in Christ. There is plenty of time to marvel in this good news because we aren't forced to cram it all in on one day. We are given time to notice where new life is springing up around us and inside of us. Easter is the season of learning how to live a new kind of life, called resurrection. *May you experience the joy, the freedom, and the excitement of new life in these days.*

Easter Sunday
Celebrate

Scripture: John 20:1-18

RESURRECTION IS THE best thing we can imagine, and celebration seems to be the only response that makes sense. This week, take notice of and celebrate the good and abundant gifts of God around you. Celebrate by throwing a party, dancing to the radio, singing in your car, or eating your favorite meal with friends. Look for every opportunity to tell stories of God's goodness. Don't be embarrassed by your joy or exuberance!

Date(s) Used:_____

What did I learn about myself and/or God in this practice?

Second Sunday of Easter
Speak Peace to Fear

Scripture: John 20:19-31

EVEN AFTER JESUS'S resurrection, his disciples were filled with fear. Each time Jesus comes to them he greets them with, "Peace!" The greatest thing to fear is death, but resurrection has even rendered that powerless. A life of resurrection carries peace, even in places of fear. This week, notice where there is fear in your home, in your workplace, in your neighborhood, and even within yourself. Ask the Holy Spirit to speak peace to you and to enable you to speak peace to others.

Date(s) Used: _____

What did I learn about myself and/or God in this practice?

Third Sunday of Easter
Look for Jesus

Scripture: Luke 24:13-35

LIKE THE DISCIPLES on the road, we often don't recognize Jesus when he is with us. Although Jesus is not present to us in body, he continues to come to us in all kinds of ways. We often expect to encounter him through Scripture, but this week we will look for Jesus everywhere, even in the stranger on the road. Sometimes we too can feel "our hearts burning within us" (Luke 24:32), but much of the time we can recognize Jesus's presence in inexplicable peace, unexpected hope, a redemptive conversation, a change of heart, a compassionate act, or a call for justice. As you look for Jesus, pay attention to where you find him. You may even want to write it down and ask how he is inviting you to respond.

Date(s) Used: _____

What did I learn about myself and/or God in this practice?

_____
_____
_____
_____
_____
_____

Fourth Sunday of Easter
Pray Psalm 23

Scripture: John 10:1-16

SINCE WE DO not have experience being sheep, it can be hard to know what it means for Jesus to be our shepherd. This week, set aside at least thirty minutes to pray Psalm 23 as a way to experience Jesus as a shepherd. As you read, imagine yourself as one of the sheep under the shepherd's care. What does it feel like to be led to still waters, to be made to lie down in green grass, or to have someone restore your soul? What is it like to follow your shepherd through a place of danger, even death—but not be afraid? How do you respond to someone leading you like this? While you imagine, allow yourself to ask your shepherd questions as they come up. What do you want to know or say? What do you want to ask for? When you have asked all your questions, ask one more: Jesus, my Good Shepherd, what is it you want to do for me? Take time to listen and receive the care of your shepherd. After your prayer time is over, write down anything you want to remember from this experience.

Date(s) Used: _____

What did I learn about myself and/or God in this practice?

_____
_____
_____
_____
_____
_____

Fifth Sunday of Easter
Practicing the Ministry of Countenance

Scripture: *1 Peter 2:2-10*

ONE OF OUR greatest means of communication is our face. The way we look at the world and at people says a lot about what we think and what we value. An encouraging, peaceful countenance can offer blessing to someone without any words being said. But this practice is not about looking happy all the time. Fake or forced happiness does nothing to show others the goodness of God. Rather, this is a practice of awareness, as we become aware of whom we're with and what our face is saying. It is also a practice of presence, being fully present in mind, body, and spirit wherever we are. Finally, it is a practice of examination, as we notice what is happening in our minds and hearts as it shows up on our face. The more time we spend basking in God's wonderful light, the more it will shine on our faces.

Date(s) Used:_____

What did I learn about myself and/or God in this practice?

Sixth Sunday of Easter
Prepare Your Story

Scripture: 1 Peter 3:13-22

IF SOMEONE WERE to ask you about the hope they see in you, what would you say? Most of us do not have a prepared answer, nor do we really expect the question. This week, spend some time thinking about how you would tell your own story of coming to life in God. If you have never recorded it for yourself, write it down. You may be surprised that your story is instructive for you even before it is for others. And, once your story is ready, be prepared to share it. If you're not sure what your story is, use these questions to guide you:

- When did you first experience God's love, and how did you respond to it?
- How has God done something for or in you that you could not have done yourself?
- Think back to one of your most difficult experiences. What got you through it?
- How have you experienced God's hope, healing, or power?
- Why do you choose to live life with God?

Date(s) Used:_____

What did I learn about myself and/or God in this practice?

HOLY DAYS: ASCENSION, PENTECOST, TRINITY SUNDAY

On Pentecost Sunday, we love to tell and retell the story of the Holy Spirit coming to the disciples in the upper room. Ascension Sunday and Trinity Sunday, on the other hand, are lesser kno,wn and, frankly, just not as exciting. But the observance of each day shapes us further into the way of Jesus as we encounter mystery, power, and a reality beyond our comprehension or control.

Ascension Sunday is the final Sunday in the season of Easter, and it marks the day that Christ ascended into heaven. We are reminded that Jesus did not remain on earth to continue a limited human existence in one place at one time. Rather, he ascended into the heavenly realm, where his presence and authority extend throughout all time and space. Observing this day gives us opportunity to consider this mystery, even if it doesn't offer many answers.

After Jesus's ascension, he gave the disciples a command to pray and wait for the Holy Spirit, who would act as an advocate, teacher, and comforter. On Pentecost Sunday, we remember when the Holy Spirit did indeed come as an unexpected mighty wind and fire—tangible evidence of God's presence from Israel's earliest days. This event is what we celebrate as the birthday of the church, when the disciples were empowered to preach in all kinds of languages and thousands believed the gospel of Jesus Christ.

On Trinity Sunday, we explore yet another mystery that will carry us through the rest of the year. There is no one scripture that specifically teaches us the doctrine of the Trinity. But early in the church's existence, as they

ruminated on Jesus's teachings and their own experiences, Christians began to recognize the three persons of God as Father, Son, and Spirit.

During these weeks of pondering mystery and power, our practices help us remember that we are only recipients of God's miraculous works. *May we receive, and may we respond in obedience.*

Ascension Sunday/ Seventh Sunday of Easter
Pray for a Different Church

Scripture: Acts 1:6-14

TRAGICALLY, "UNITY" IS not the first word that comes to mind when people are asked about Christians. We often allow differences to bring division and end up competing against one another rather than cheering one another on. This week, spend time learning about and praying for a church in your area that isn't your own. Especially look for a church of a different language or ethnic group. Drive by the church building, visit the website, or find out if you know anyone who is part of that church. See what you can learn about what they are doing, how they are seeking to serve the community, and who attends their church. Pray earnestly that God would use this congregation to further God's kingdom and produce good fruit in your community. Pray for their pastor(s) by name, maybe even writing it in a note or an email. As you pray for this church, pray also that Jesus's own prayer for unity among his church would be answered.

Date(s) Used: _____

What did I learn about myself and/or God in this practice?

Pentecost Sunday
Silence

Scripture: Acts 2:1-21

BEFORE THE SOUND of mighty rushing wind and the cacophony of multiple languages being spoken at the same time, there was silence. The Spirit came in the quiet moments of the disciples' waiting. This week we will also wait for the Holy Spirit as we practice five minutes of silence a day. Choose a time of day that will be free of interruptions, perhaps first thing in the morning. Set an alarm or timer so you do not have to watch the time. Sit in silence for five full minutes without reading, writing, or listening to anything. Do not be alarmed if your mind jumps around to a million different things during this time. Be persistent in putting these things to rest, making space for God to speak into your stillness. Be reminded of God's presence, and ask for even greater awareness of the Spirit's work in you.

Date(s) Used: _____

What did I learn about myself and/or God in this practice?

_____
_____
_____
_____
_____
_____

Trinity Sunday
Five Names

Scripture: Matthew 28:16-20

THIS WEEK, WE will practice Jesus's Commission to make disciples by praying for people who do not yet know the hope of life with Christ. Spend some time prayerfully creating a list of five names of people whom you know are not living abundant life with God. Once a day, pray with your list for five minutes, spending at least one minute on each name. Pray that God would reveal himself to them, that they would know they are loved, and that they would find freedom in Christ. As you pray, be open to hear ways that the Spirit may ask you to write a note, send an invitation, or initiate a conversation with someone you pray for. But do not feel pressure to do anything besides pray; remember that the Spirit is the one who reveals, teaches, and convicts.

Date(s) Used:_____

What did I learn about myself and/or God in this practice?

ORDINARY TIME

It seems significant that Trinity Sunday is our entryway into the longest "non-season season" of the Christian calendar: Ordinary Time. Like the doctrine of the Trinity, which the church discovered through the ordinary ebbs and flows of life, so in Ordinary Time we learn to walk with Jesus in the days that go unmarked and unnamed.

The seasons of Advent, Christmas, Epiphany, Lent, and Easter heighten our awareness for what God is doing in the world, but the months in Ordinary Time can have a way of dulling our awareness. The summer and back-to-school months also bring disruptions to our schedules with travel and vacations, followed by a flurry of activity to get back into gear. If we are not careful, we can check out altogether until, suddenly, it's time for Advent again!

If we learn to pay attention, however, we will find that some of the most ordinary things are actually extraordinary things that we just get used to because they happen all the time. The days grow longer and then shorter again as evidences of our planet's movement around the sun. Seeds—once just tiny bits buried in soil—grow into beautiful flowers, sweet fruit, and nourishing vegetables. Our playgrounds echo with the sounds of shrieks and laughter. Bike paths and lakes and sidewalks fill with people enjoying God's good creation. The wonders of Ordinary Time are all around us.

And in these wonders of Ordinary Time, we are invited into a new experience of our triune God at work. While the seasons invite us to walk through the story of Jesus, we now have opportunity to notice how Jesus is walking with us. We find freedom to explore the particular themes of our own journey as we discern the Spirit's guidance in the very ordinary activities of life.

The Lectionary offers scheduled texts for each Sunday in Ordinary Time, but the Ordinary Time practices in this book are organized by theme rather than scriptural text. Using the freedom and discernment of Ordinary Time, you can hop and skip around, choosing a pattern of practices that best fits your own journey through these weeks. Directly following the Ordinary Time section is one that contains practices designed for specific events that may occur during our observance of Ordinary Time, or at any other time throughout the year. These events and the practices for them include election day, vacation, and tragedy.

The practices of Ordinary Time are designed to help us partner with the Spirit in growing good fruit in ourselves. *May you be aware of God in all the ordinary places, and may you know comfort and peace as Jesus walks with you there.*

EPHESIANS: PRACTICING RESURRECTION

The following eight practices are based on readings from the book of Ephesians, which Eugene Peterson suggested is our primer for practicing resurrection. If you are not using another plan for daily reading, you may want to read through Ephesians along with these practices.

Practicing Resurrection
Gratitude

"He has showered his kindness on us, along with all wisdom and understanding."
—Ephesians 1:8, NLT

WHEN WE THINK of all we have been given, gratitude is the only response that makes sense. This week, practice gratitude by keeping a running list of all you are grateful for, starting with the gifts of God listed in Ephesians 1. But your list doesn't only have to include obviously spiritual things; feel free to include a special neighbor, ice cream, coffee, your dog—whatever you receive as good gifts. As a goal, try to list 100 things this week, but don't be surprised if you go over!

Date(s) Used: _____

What did I learn about myself and/or God in this practice?

Practicing Resurrection
Be a Person of Peace

"For Christ himself has brought peace to us. He united Jews and Gentiles into one people when, in his own body on the cross, he broke down the wall of hostility that separated us."

—Ephesians 2:14, NLT

THE WALLS THAT divide us by political party, race, language, socioeconomic standing, and ideology are easy to build and maintain. But the peace of Christ breaks down these barriers, and we are invited into this work of peacemaking as well. This week, be a person of peace by consciously looking for, working toward, and celebrating peace everywhere you go. If you hear or read a divisive conversation, work to steer it toward peace. When you are offended, pray first that Jesus would bring you peace and enable you to bring that peace to others.

Date(s) Used:_____

What did I learn about myself and/or God in this practice?

Practicing Resurrection
Pray for Others

"Make every effort to keep yourselves united in the Spirit, binding yourselves together with peace."

—Ephesians 4:3, NLT

THIS WEEK, WE will pray for others as our primary effort in keeping ourselves united in the Spirit. Early in the week, ask the Lord to help you know for whom you are to pray. Make a short list of names, churches, or other organizations. Some names on this list might include individuals outside your close circle of friends and family; a church or ministry that you drive by regularly; people in your congregation; or neighbors in your community or near your church. Whenever you pray for these names, take time to think about what God wants for this person or group of people. Ask the Lord to richly bless them and to make his good and perfect desires come true for them.

Date(s) Used: _____

What did I learn about myself and/or God in this practice?

Practicing Resurrection
Daily Scripture Reading & Dialogue

"Then we will no longer be immature like children. We won't be tossed and blown about by every wind of new teaching. We will not be influenced when people try to trick us with lies so clever they sound like the truth."

—Ephesians 4:14, NLT

WE GROW UP as we learn, read, ask questions, and wrestle out the answers in our lives among others. This week, participate in this process by reading Scripture every day, following your own reading plan or reading in Ephesians. But don't keep what you read to yourself. Look for ways you can participate in dialogue with the Spirit and with other believers about what you read. What questions does it raise? How does it challenge or affirm you? How does it lead you to pray, or to action? Submit to the guidance of the Divine Helper—the Holy Spirit—and engage in conversations with others for encouragement as well.

Date(s) Used:_____

What did I learn about myself and/or God in this practice?

Practicing Resurrection
Waking Up

"For the light makes everything visible. This is why it is said, 'Awake, O sleeper, rise up from the dead, and Christ will give you light.'"

—Ephesians 5:14, NLT

THIS WEEK, USE the process of waking up as a way to practice resurrection. Be intentional as you move from sleep into your day. Here are some ideas to help you:

- See if you can make prayer your first conscious act. Ask God for knowledge of his presence as you begin the day.
- As you move through your morning routine, look for opportunities to invite God in. Talk to Jesus about the events of the day ahead or about memories from the day before.
- Write a scriptural reminder or a word of encouragement for yourself the night before. Post it on your bathroom mirror or near your coffee pot to help guide your thoughts early in the morning.

Date(s) Used:_____

What did I learn about myself and/or God in this practice?

Ordinary Time

Practicing Resurrection
Three Blessings

"Out of respect for Christ, be courteously reverent to one another."
—Ephesians 5:21, MSG

YEAR A

THIS WEEK, WE will practice giving three blessings as a way to revere Christ as well as those around us. With prayerful intention and planning, choose three actions that will bless someone else. You might write a note of encouragement, buy someone's lunch, give an unexpected gift, or simply show up and have conversation with a person who usually sits alone. If and when you are tempted to shrug off the work of blessing others, allow Christ's love and blessing to you fuel your desire to bless others.

Date(s) Used: _____

What did I learn about myself and/or God in this practice?

Practicing Resurrection
Breath Prayer

"Pray in the Spirit at all times and on every occasion. Stay alert and be persistent in your prayers for all believers everywhere."

—Ephesians 6:18, NLT

THERE IS MUCH to distract us in twenty-first-century life, and it can be difficult to stay alert and persistent in prayer. This week, replace usual distractions with the practice of breath prayer. Notice when you feel the need to check out by picking up your phone, turning on the TV or radio, or flipping through a magazine. Instead of distracting yourself, settle into the moment and pray a simple prayer in rhythm with your exhalation and inhalation. Try one of these breath prayers, or use your own:

- Be still (*inhale*), and know that I am God (*exhale*).
- The Lord is my shepherd (*inhale*); I shall not want (*exhale*).

Date(s) Used: _____

What did I learn about myself and/or God in this practice?

_____
_____
_____
_____
_____

Ordinary Time

Practicing Resurrection
Sabbath Rest

"Peace be with you, dear brothers and sisters, and may God the Father and the Lord Jesus Christ give you love with faithfulness."

—Ephesians 6:23, NLT

SABBATH IS A twenty-four-hour practice of *shalom*: peaceful, restful, well-being that is given as a gift to God's people. It is not a reward for finishing all our work; rather, it is an interruption of our work so we can receive what we need from our God, who is always working for our good. Plan ahead to take one day off from everything you possibly can: errands, cooking, cleaning, driving, to-do lists, obligations, or appointments. Use the time to see how much "nothing" you can do. You have permission to be lazy. Take a nap—or several. Receive rest as a gift from this God who restores your soul.

Date(s) Used:_____

What did I learn about myself and/or God in this practice?

NURTURING THE FRUIT OF THE SPIRIT

It is the Spirit's work to grow good fruit in us, but we can engage in practices that either encourage or hinder that work. Use the next eighteen practices to partner with God as the Spirit grows good, beautiful fruit in you.

Love, Joy, and Peace
Asking for Awareness

IN THE MUNDANE details of our own lives, it can be difficult to remember that we are part of God's life. While we keep busy and entertained, it can be hard to see how we are part of God's grand story. This week, pray daily for a growing awareness of God's presence, purpose, and activity within and around you. Place this prayer in a prominent place and pray it as often as you see it: *Lord, I know I am part of your life. Give me the gift of awareness to notice, see, hear, and experience where you are and what you are doing. Amen.*

Date(s) Used: _____

What did I learn about myself and/or God in this practice?

_____
_____
_____
_____
_____
_____

Love, Joy, and Peace
Counting Up Redemption

"So you also should consider yourselves to be dead to the power of sin and alive to God through Christ Jesus."

—Romans 6:11, NLT

IN THIS VERSE, the word translated as "count" (NIV), "consider" (NLT), or sometimes "reckon" (KJV/NKJV) is an accounting term in Greek. It has the connotation of adding up a sum to know what you already have. This is an action we take to understand and live into the reality of what has happened in us. This week, take time to consider your salvation during one of your daily routines, like making coffee, driving to work, or packing a lunch. Each time you engage in that activity, rehearse the reality of what God has done in you through Christ. Take time to count up the balance you've been given, and spend the rest of the day living with the knowledge of who you are now and where you stand.

Date(s) Used:_____

What did I learn about myself and/or God in this practice?

Love, Joy, and Peace
Making Amends

THE TWELVE STEPS of recovery used in Alcoholics Anonymous are powerful tools for change. Steps 8 and 9 of the Twelve Steps are:

> 8. *We made a list of all persons we had harmed and became willing to make amends to them all.*
> 9. *We made direct amends to such people whenever possible, except when to do so would injure them or others.*

This week, allow the Spirit to guide you through these practices. Be aware that becoming willing to make amends is a process of its own, and it's okay if you're not there yet. Making amends may include a spoken or written apology, returning something that was stolen, or simply giving up a grudge you've been holding. For those in recovery, these steps are taken with the help of a sponsor. This can be difficult, so don't feel the need to do it alone. A pastor or trusted Christian friend may be a necessary companion on this journey.

Date(s) Used: _____

What did I learn about myself and/or God in this practice?

Love, Joy, and Peace
Listen to Words of Love

YEAR A

HADEWIJCH OF ANTWERP was a member of the Beguines, a medieval renewal movement of women (c. 1200, Belgium) who formed communities of worship and mutual economic support. Though renowned for their zeal in prayer and their charitable works, several were pronounced heretics, and even executed, for their mystical teachings. Hadewijch wrote essays and poetry about her experience of God's love, which empowered her obedience. Use her words this week to reflect on your own experience of God's love and your response.

Love is always new!
Those who live in Love are renewed every day
And through their frequent acts of goodness
Are born all over again.
How can anyone stay old in Love's presence?
How can anyone be timid there?

Date(s) Used:_____

What did I learn about myself and/or God in this practice?

Love, Joy, and Peace
Worship

"And they sang in a mighty chorus: 'Worthy is the Lamb who was slaughtered—to receive power and riches and wisdom and strength and honor and glory and blessing.'"

—Revelation 5:12, NLT

WORSHIP IS MORE than what we do when we gather on Sundays. Worship is a spiritual practice of seeing and naming God's great worth. This week, plan to spend at least five minutes each day in conscious, active worship, dwelling upon and expressing God's greatness. If you're not sure how to start, use Revelation 5:12–13 as a guide.

Date(s) Used:_____

What did I learn about myself and/or God in this practice?

_____

_____

_____

_____

_____

_____

_____

Love, Joy, and Peace
Daily Examen

IT IS OFTEN easier to recognize God's action in hindsight than in the moment. This week, we will practice the discipline of Daily Examen as a way to notice the presence and invitation of God in our lives. We look back on the previous day, rummaging through our "stuff," and find God in it—sometimes in the most unexpected places. To practice the Examen this week, set aside three to five minutes at the same time every day. Use these steps to guide your reflection.

1. Ask the Holy Spirit to join you as you review events of the last twenty-four hours.
2. Focus on the day's gifts and give thanks for them.
3. Notice what emotions you felt. What is God saying to you in these feelings?
4. Ask the Spirit to guide you to one particular event or emotion of the day that is important, and pray repentance, gratitude, or a request/petition accordingly.
5. Ask for the Lord's light to shine on tomorrow's events and decisions.

Date(s) Used:_____

What did I learn about myself and/or God in this practice?

Patience, Kindness, and Goodness
Learning to Wait

FEW OF US (if any) enjoy waiting, but we do it a lot: we wait in traffic, in the drive-thru, for a promised raise, for test results, for kids to put their shoes on, for God to move. This week, notice what you do when you are waiting. If you get aggravated, ask yourself why. Use it as an opportunity for conversation with God about the circumstance or about your own impatience. Remind yourself that waiting may be an opportunity to increase your desire and capacity to receive.

Date(s) Used:_____

Ordinary Time

What did I learn about myself and/or God in this practice?

Patience, Kindness, and Goodness
Generosity

WE ARE SURROUNDED by and inundated with a myth of scarcity, or the idea that we must protect what we have because there is not enough to go around. As people living in God's kingdom, though, we are ruled not by scarcity but by *abundance*. God has more than enough, and he shares it freely. Everything we have has been given to us. It is all "manna," given to us daily by our more-than-generous God. God's provision makes it possible for us to be generous as well, no matter how much we have. This week, practice generosity as you buy someone's coffee, give to a ministry, or get a grocery gift card for a neighbor who needs it. As you do, be reminded of and grateful for the ways God has been generous toward you.

Date(s) Used:_____

What did I learn about myself and/or God in this practice?

Patience, Kindness, and Goodness
Meet a Neighbor

THIS WEEK, BE intentional about meeting a neighbor you don't know yet. If this idea makes you nervous, remember that it doesn't have to be a long conversation, and it doesn't need to end with a prayer. Look for a time when you can introduce yourself and learn about him or her. It may be five minutes or fewer. Typical neighborly interactions in today's culture tend to be limited to smiling and waving to one another as we drive away. But make it your goal to be able to call your neighbors by name. Pray that God continues to open doors and guide conversations. You may be surprised by the opportunities you find to be a good neighbor!

Ordinary Time

Date(s) Used: _____

What did I learn about myself and/or God in this practice?

Patience, Kindness, and Goodness
Help in Real Ways

WE ARE ACCUSTOMED to saying polite things like, "I'll be praying for you," or, "I'm sorry; I hope things get better." Those kinds of comments and sentiments are certainly not bad! But this week, when you are confronted with a neighbor's need, go a step further than the typical response. Look for a tangible, appropriate way to help the person in need. Stop and offer to pray with the person on the spot rather than praying privately (or forgetting) later. Even if it's an inconvenience, offer a ride, bring a meal, or look for the lost cat yourself—rather than hoping someone else will do it.

Date(s) Used:_____

What did I learn about myself and/or God in this practice?

Patience, Kindness, and Goodness
Learning to Trust

MOTHER TERESA, NOW known as Saint Teresa of Calcutta, was born in 1910 in Macedonia, and died in 1997. As a young woman, she moved to India, where she loved and cared for the very poor and sick of Calcutta, India. In 1950, she established the Missionaries of Charity, a Catholic religious order now comprising more than five thousand sisters. Someone once asked Mother Teresa to pray that they would have clarity. Her response was: "I will not do that. Clarity is that last thing you are clinging to and must let go of. I have never had clarity; what I have always had is trust. So I will pray that you trust God." This week, take the words of St. Teresa with you as you pray. Whenever you are seeking answers from God, turn your heart's desire to learning to trust God.

Date(s) Used:_____

What did I learn about myself and/or God in this practice?

Ordinary Time

Patience, Kindness, and Goodness
Serve in Secret

YEAR A

AS WE WALK the way of Jesus, we are invited into the new creation patterns of love, blessing, and self-sacrifice. But the old ways of pride, manipulation, and self-centeredness can creep in even as we strive to do good for others. This week, practice serving others in secret, knowing that your only reward will be from your Father, who sees everything we do. Experience the joy of putting other people's needs before your own: do someone's laundry; pull a neighbor's weeds; wash someone's car; show up to serve at a compassionate ministry; send an anonymous note of encouragement. You may not be able to keep it totally secret, and that's okay. When you're found out, don't seek or bask in credit. Give a simple, humble response, and move on.

Date(s) Used:_____

What did I learn about myself and/or God in this practice?

Faithfulness, Gentleness, and Self-Control
Tell a God Story

WHEN HAVE YOU experienced a God story? Think about a time you experienced miraculous provision, received clear guidance, or witnessed God's astonishing activity. Look for an opportunity to tell this story to someone this week. When we retell these experiences, we are reminded all over again of God's goodness. Our God stories bring us joy, nurture our trust, and encourage others. You will be surprised at what telling a story can do!

Date(s) Used: _____

What did I learn about myself and/or God in this practice?

_____
_____
_____
_____
_____
_____

Ordinary Time

Faithfulness, Gentleness, and Self-Control
Partnering with God

IN HIS BOOK *Garden City,* John Mark Comer reminds us that we are not God's *employees* but God's *coworkers* in bringing about the restoration of the world. This week, whether you work as a lawyer, teacher, physician, foreman, IT tech, farmer, stay-at-home parent, or something else—as you do whatever your work in this world is, do it as God's partner. If it's hard for you to see how your work moves God's creation project forward, ask the Spirit to show you.

Date(s) Used: _____

What did I learn about myself and/or God in this practice?

Faithfulness, Gentleness, and Self-Control
Praying "Your Kingdom Come"

JESUS HAS INSTRUCTED us to pray, "Your kingdom come, your will be done, on earth as it is in heaven" (Matthew 6.10). When we pray this, we are asking that God would have full authority as King to do whatever he wants, however he wants. And the first piece of earth where we are asking God to be King is *in us*. This week, pray this prayer as often as you can. You may want to write it on a card and place it somewhere you will see it often. Be prepared to hear from the Spirit regarding places within you where God is not King.

Date(s) Used: _____

What did I learn about myself and/or God in this practice?

Faithfulness, Gentleness, and Self-Control
The Art of Listening

WE HEAR A lot of sounds, but we rarely take the time to *listen*. In our daily lives, there is so much that demands our attention that we rarely listen to one another. Or we are too busy getting someone to listen to us that we don't find time to listen to them. But when we do listen, we may be surprised by what we hear and what we are invited to participate in. This week, intentionally practice listening by doing some or all of the following:

- Remind yourself that faces are more important than screens. Every time a person is in front of you, look at that person instead of your TV, phone, or computer.
- Don't talk over people. While in conversation, make an effort to think about what the other person is saying rather than trying to figure out what you're going to say next.
- Pay attention to your body language. Make eye contact, uncross your arms, and lean forward.
- Repeat/clarify what you've heard by saying, "I think what you're saying is . . ." Checking for clarification communicates that you really want to understand the other person.

Date(s) Used: _____

What did I learn about myself and/or God in this practice?

Faithfulness, Gentleness, and Self-Control
Solitude

SOLITUDE IS THE practice of hospitality to oneself, and it is necessary in order to be able to offer true hospitality to anyone else. This time alone is the first place we learn to make space for ourselves and for God. This week, practice small amounts of solitude daily (fifteen to twenty minutes), or choose one day to spend at least one full hour in solitude. During this time, do not listen to music, read books, watch TV, or scroll through social media. This is time to be fully present to yourself and have a conversation with God about what you think and feel. Resist the urge to jump into action; practice simply noticing what's going on in you. Afterward, take some time to reflect on your experience. What was challenging, freeing, comforting, intriguing? How well do you create space for yourself and for others?

Date(s) Used:_____

What did I learn about myself and/or God in this practice?

Faithfulness, Gentleness, and Self-Control
Creating Margin

WE OFTEN THINK that better means more, but abundant life with God is not about doing more. In fact, it might be about doing less. As we participate in God's life, we can create space for God, family, rest, and leisure as we practice creating margin in our lives. This week, examine your daily activities and weekly routines. Are you living life all the way to the edge of your time and resources? How can you create some white space—some margin—around the edges?

Date(s) Used:_____

What did I learn about myself and/or God in this practice?

PRACTICES FOR NOT-SO-ORDINARY TIME: VACATION, ELECTIONS, TRAGEDY

In the midst of Ordinary Time there are often weeks that feel anything but ordinary. Vacation is a planned escape from the ordinary, while tragic events come unexpectedly and uproot all sense of normalcy. And, for those who follow the news closely, election season often has a life all its own. Find these practices when you need them, and use them to connect you to the God who is unchanging but certainly not ordinary.

A Practice for Vacation
Play

JOY IS A natural product of the resurrected life. But sometimes we need to *remember* the joy that is ours, and playing is a great way to do that. While you are on vacation, treat play as a serious spiritual practice. Make plans to spend time doing things that bring you joy. Play is something that doesn't feel productive, and it's often something that makes you lose track of time. If play doesn't feel very spiritual to you, pray before, during, or after that the Holy Spirit would help you see God in your play.

Date(s) Used: _____

What did I learn about myself and/or God in this practice?

A Practice for Election Season
Vote with Care

JOHN WESLEY RECORDED in his journal on October 6, 1774: *"I met those of our society who had votes in the ensuing election, and advised them 1. To vote, without fee or reward, for the person they judged most worthy 2. To speak no evil of the person they voted against, and 3. To take care their spirits were not sharpened against those that voted on the other side."* This week, take these old but relevant words with you as you vote, read the news, and observe/participate in social media. If you cannot enter into a conversation (whether in person or online) without violating the last two points, it may be better not to have the conversation at all. Even in these polarizing times, we can do as Wesley encourages because the recipient of our ultimate allegiance and hope is not someone who depends on anyone's vote.

Date(s) Used: _____

What did I learn about myself and/or God in this practice?

Not-so-Ordinary Time

A Practice during Tragedy
Defying Death

WHEN TRAGEDY STRIKES, we are instantly reminded that death wields tremendous power. And the death sin brings can be seen everywhere we look: oppression, deceit, abuse, fear, shame, war, poverty, injustice, despair. These forces that rip lives apart seem so powerful and so final. But for those who are in Christ, devastating forces do not have final say over us! This week, whenever you are confronted with one of these or other forms of death, make an intentional practice to remind yourself that death does not have the last word. When you feel overwhelmed, imagine yourself as you are: with Christ, who has defied and will forever defy death.

Date(s) Used:_____

What did I learn about myself and/or God in this practice?

CHRIST THE KING SUNDAY

Christ the King Sunday is the final Sunday of Ordinary Time, before the church year begins anew with Advent. Once again, we will grow in hopeful anticipation as we learn to wait in the dark. But if we're not careful, we could be fooled into thinking that all we have to hope for and expect is the presents, the decadent food, or the glittering decorations of our Christmas celebrations.

Christ the King Sunday offers us a clear picture of what we expectantly await during Advent—our King and his kingdom to come on earth, even as it is in heaven. We are reminded that our King is unlike any other king, and his kingdom unlike any other kingdom. So we should not be surprised if we find ourselves becoming unlike other people.

In this week before Advent, we enter a kind of preparation before the preparation. *Let us fix our eyes on King Jesus, and may we find our home in his kingdom.*

Christ the King Sunday
Daily Silence

Scripture: Matthew 25:31-46

WE ARE TURNING the corner into Advent, the season in which we anticipate Christ's coming. But we cannot anticipate that of which we are not aware. If we can cultivate awareness of what God is doing, we will naturally respond in love, joy, anticipation, and obedience. But busyness, worry, stress, and entertainment compete to crowd out and dull our awareness of God. So, before the busyness of the coming season gets to you, take time to focus your attention on what is most important. You may even find you want to carry this practice through the season of Advent. This week, carve out some space for awareness in your mind, heart, and body by practicing at least five minutes of silence each day. Set an alarm on your phone or computer to remind you each day. If you are ready to deepen this practice, spend ten or even fifteen minutes in silence each day. To help still your mind, you may repeat this simple prayer: *"Holy Spirit, open my eyes and my heart to see you and to want you."*

Date(s) Used: _____

What did I learn about myself and/or God in this practice?

YEAR B

THE SEASON OF ADVENT

We often assume Advent is the countdown to Christmas: the church equivalent of how many shopping days we have left. The season does begin four Sundays prior to Christmas Day, but we aren't preparing ourselves for Christ coming as a baby. Instead, Advent is the preparation of people who live in the in-between: looking back on Christ's birth, and looking forward to when Christ will come again.

As a result, the scriptures of Advent feel decidedly un-Christmasy. They are filled with prophetic words of judgment against oppressive earthly powers and proclamations of the justice and peace that will replace these powers in God's kingdom. Advent is not so much a season of light and hope as a season of waiting in the dark.

It is significant that the Christian calendar begins this way. We begin the year in an honest place, admitting that we do, in fact, need saving, and that the One who saves chooses to do it in a different way than we expect.

In these weeks, we do not celebrate the God who comes to us on *our* schedule, conforming to *our* list of requirements. In Advent, we recognize that God comes to us not in the way or timeline we *expect* but in the way we *need*. The best things—forming new life, making people whole, restoring the world—cannot be rushed.

During this season, we will take on practices that help us prepare our hearts and minds for this God who comes to us. *May we grow in awareness, trust, and expectation of our God as we wait in the dark.*

First Sunday of Advent
Sabbath

Scripture: Mark 13:24-37

MANY OF US live in a perpetual state of exhaustion and busyness, which makes it difficult to be aware and alert. This week we will practice Sabbath, which interrupts our lives as one full day without work, dedicated to rest and play. If you cannot practice Sabbath for an entire twenty-four-hour period, carve out at least six hours in one day for this practice. Keep these things in mind as you practice Sabbath:

- Do not do anything that feels like work or that is on any of your to-do lists.
- Spend time doing things that truly restore and energize you.
- Be aware that many things function to distract us but usually do not help to restore us (e.g., entertainment, social media, shopping).
- Some suggested activities include sleep, play, feasting, time with family and friends, reading, celebration, and time outdoors.

Date(s) Used: _____

What did I learn about myself and/or God in this practice?

_____
_____
_____
_____
_____
_____

Second Sunday of Advent
Prepare and Share a Meal

Scripture: Mark 1:1-8

IN THE MIDST of busy and hectic schedules, many of us spend as little time preparing food as possible. We eat quickly and get on to whatever happens next. This week, practice meal preparation as a way to think about, care for, and have conversations with those nearest to us. Here are some ideas to help put this into practice:

- If you live alone, invite a friend, neighbor, or family member to join you for a meal this week. If that's not possible, prepare a meal and bring it to someone.
- If you do not usually do the cooking in your family, offer to cook one night or pack lunch(es) for your family members.
- For families, choose at least one night this week to sit down to a meal together. Engage all family members in preparation: making the food, setting the table, getting drinks, maybe even lighting candles on the table.

During your preparation, think about the ways God has prepared his good gifts for us. Ask the Lord what it might mean for you to prepare the way for him.

Date(s) Used: _____

What did I learn about myself and/or God in this practice?

Third Sunday of Advent
Clear Media Distraction

Scripture: John 1:6-8, 19-28

THIS WEEK, PARTICIPATE in a partial media fast as you seek to clear a path for the Lord in your life. You can do this one of several ways:

- Choose one form of media to fast all week, such as TV, movies, streaming channels, social media, video games, radio, magazines, and/or news.
- Choose at least one day to fast from all media.
- Fast from any media that draws you away from the work of God in your life. This allows you to focus on music, art, shows, and performances that help you further engage with the seasons of Advent and Christmas.

Date(s) Used: _____

What did I learn about myself and/or God in this practice?

_____
_____
_____
_____
_____
_____

Fourth Sunday of Advent
Phone-Free Day

Scripture: Luke 1:26-38

IT IS DIFFICULT to say yes to God's invitation if we are too distracted to hear it. This week, practice at least one phone-free day. For most of us, our smartphones are not just a way to talk to others but also a way to work when we're not at work, compare our lives with others, and distract ourselves when we're bored. Choose one day this week to be completely without your phone. Here are some ideas to help you in this practice:

- Notify people in advance that you cannot be reached that day.
- Every time your fingers get fidgety and want to scroll something, take it as an invitation to be more fully present in your surroundings.
- Use your time to take a walk, start a conversation, take a nap, or just enjoy the silence.

Date(s) Used:_____

What did I learn about myself and/or God in this practice?

THE TWELVE DAYS OF CHRISTMAS

For most American Evangelical Christians, what we know of the twelve days of Christmas is from a song—of which the only words we all know for sure are "FIVE GOLDEN RINGS!" But for most of the history of the church, Christmas has been celebrated for twelve full days, from December 25 through January 5. This short season ends with the commemoration of the Epiphany of the Magi on January 6, which ushers in the much longer season of Epiphany.

During the twelve days of Christmas, we take time to appreciate the wonder of the incarnation: God who comes to dwell with us, becoming like us. It is a season decidedly opposed to the consumer mentality that engulfs a typical American Christmas celebration. Christ is not just one of the gifts we unwrap in a hurry and forget about a few days later. These days give us time to savor, enjoy, and bask in the goodness that is God-with-us.

Christmas Day and Epiphany are always the same dates: December 25 and January 6. Because these dates fall on different days of the week each year, there may not always be two Sundays within the twelve days of Christmas. The Sunday on or immediately following January 6 is celebrated as Epiphany Sunday.

May these days of Christmas be full of joy as we receive the God who comes to us.

Christmas Day or First Sunday after Christmas
Reflection

Scripture: Luke 2:22-40

MANY OF US make resolutions at the beginning of a new year. But before you make plans for the coming year, take some time this week to reflect on the year behind you. Specifically reflect on who has spoken into your life as a Simeon or an Anna. Who has provided prophetic words of hope and meaning for you? Remember what they have said, ponder what it means for you, and give thanks for them. As you do, you may find that your reflection guides your own resolutions and decisions for the new year.

Date(s) Used:_____

What did I learn about myself and/or God in this practice?

Second Sunday of Christmas or Epiphany Sunday
Inclusion

Scripture: Ephesians 3:1-12

THE HOLIDAY SEASON can be a joyful time spent with family and close friends. But for many it is an incredibly lonely and sad time. This week, think of those you know who may feel especially isolated this time of year. Do you know anyone who:

- Lives far away or is estranged from their family?
- Lives alone?
- Is incarcerated or has a family member incarcerated?
- Is living in a nursing home?
- Receives long-term treatment in the hospital?

Once you have identified a person or a group, determine how you can include them in your week. You may make a phone call, take a meal, write a card, go for a visit. Whatever you do, know that you are giving a very good gift: the gift of not being alone.

Date(s) Used: _____

What did I learn about myself and/or God in this practice?

_____
_____
_____
_____
_____

THE SEASON OF EPIPHANY

Epiphany may be the season least familiar to those of us in Protestant-Evangelical traditions. Yet it might be the most wonderful season of them all, filled with light, and joy, and pure astonishment at the wonder of God.

An epiphany is defined as "an appearance or manifestation, especially of a divine being," which is an apt description of what happened when Magi from the East discovered a star that told of a newborn king. But the story of the Magi is not just about their epiphany; it's an epiphany for us too. It reminds us that God is in the business of telling people about himself, even—and maybe especially—the people we assume don't know the first thing about God. During this season we revel in the light that God shines so that any and all can see God's glory. And, like the Magi, as we encounter the dazzling beauty of this God of light, love, and power, we find that we are changed.

Epiphany begins at the same time every year but has varying lengths depending on the date of Easter. The final Sunday in Epiphany is Transfiguration Sunday. Ash Wednesday, which marks the beginning of the season of Lent, falls in the week after Transfiguration Sunday. The date of Ash Wednesday is determined by counting back six weeks from the date of Easter. For each Lectionary year (Year A, Year B, Year C), this book includes the maximum amount of potential weeks for an Epiphany season, but most years will have fewer. Transfiguration Sunday will always be the Sunday directly preceding Ash Wednesday.

During Epiphany, we will engage in practices to help us receive the light God gives us. *May we be astonished and overjoyed—both by God's dazzling light and by what God's light grows in us.*

First Sunday after Epiphany/ Baptism of the Lord
Daily Examen

Scripture: Mark 1:4-11

NOT OFTEN DO we hear a voice from heaven affirming that we are seen, loved, and valued. But God is no less present to us than he was to Jesus—if we have the awareness to notice. Sometimes it is difficult to notice God in the present moment, but the practice of Daily Examen allows us to look back on our day to see with the clarity of hindsight. To practice the Examen this week, set aside three to five minutes at the same time every day. Use these steps to guide your reflection.

1. Ask the Holy Spirit to join you as you review events of the last twenty-four hours.
2. Focus on the day's gifts and give thanks for them.
3. Notice what emotions you felt. What is God saying to you in these feelings?
4. Ask the Spirit to guide you to one particular event or emotion of the day that is important, and pray repentance, gratitude, or a request/petition accordingly.
5. Ask for the Lord's light to shine on tomorrow's events and decisions.

Date(s) Used:_____

What did I learn about myself and/or God in this practice?

Second Sunday after the Epiphany
Invite Jesus to Come Along

Scripture: 1 Corinthians 6:12-20

THIS WEEK, INVITE Jesus to come along with you wherever you go and whatever you do. Before you walk into a building, ask him to come along. Before you take a bite or drink, ask him to join you. Before you make a purchase, ask him to walk with you to the checkout. Ask him to teach you how you can honor God with your body in your regular activities. If you feel uncomfortable having Jesus do something alongside you, it might be a nudge that it is not a God-honoring activity. Use those moments to talk with Jesus about it too.

Date(s) Used: _____

What did I learn about myself and/or God in this practice?

Third Sunday after the Epiphany
Think about Better Things

Scripture: 1 Corinthians 7:29-31

IT IS EASY to become absorbed in both the troubles and the pleasures of earth. This week, practice pulling your thoughts toward what is better, and eternal. Anytime you find yourself anxious about, obsessing over, or overly attached to something—good or bad—use it as a cue to think about the astounding gift of intimacy with God. To help you in this practice, you might want to write Colossians 3:1–2 or Ephesians 1:3–4 somewhere you will see often.

Date(s) Used: _____

What did I learn about myself and/or God in this practice?

_____
_____
_____
_____
_____
_____

Fourth Sunday after the Epiphany
Not Having to Be Right

Scripture: 1 Corinthians 8:1-13

OUR CULTURE PLACES a high value on being right, and we all go to great lengths to prove to others that we are right. This week, in an effort to remember that knowledge is not the greatest virtue in God's kingdom, practice giving up your need to be right. Unless doing so would cause harm to you or someone else, let the other person have the last word when you are contradicted. Whenever the issue at hand is none other than your own desire to be right, let the argument go. If a situation really does require that you bring correction, do so with gentleness, respect, and discretion.

Date(s) Used:_____

What did I learn about myself and/or God in this practice?

Fifth Sunday after the Epiphany
Service

Scripture: 1 Corinthians 9:16-23

WHEN WE PRACTICE service, we employ our God-given resources for the benefit of others in partnership with God's work in the world. The way you serve may look very different from how another person serves. Some have avenues of service built into their vocation. But we are not serving on accident or by default. The discipline of this practice is found in the intent: purposefully engaging what we have to benefit others. If you're not sure how to start, pray these words each day and see where the Spirit leads you: *"Lord, you have given me all that I have. Show me today how I can use these gifts to serve others and honor you."*

Date(s) Used: _____

What did I learn about myself and/or God in this practice?

Sixth Sunday after the Epiphany
Exercise

Scripture: 1 Corinthians 9:24-27

WE OFTEN FORGET that our body, mind, and spirit are deeply and mysteriously connected. Physical exercise is certainly not the same thing as spiritual transformation, nor can spiritual practices replace the necessary task of caring for and strengthening our bodies. We are both body and spirit, and we must pay attention to both. This week, spend at least one hour exercising your body. If this is out of your normal routine, look for something that will get your heart rate and breathing up but is not too strenuous. You may go for a long walk or a run, use the step machine at a gym, or participate in a yoga or fitness class. If exercise is already part of your weekly routine, take care to connect your mind and heart to what your body is doing. As you stretch and strengthen your body, think about the way your mind and spirit are stretched and strengthened. What is happening in your spirit, and how is it connected to your body? Are you training for anything? Should you be training for anything? And if so, what does that need to look like?

Date(s) Used:_____

What did I learn about myself and/or God in this practice?

Seventh Sunday after the Epiphany
Just Say No

Scripture: 2 Corinthians 1:18-22

FOR MANY OF us who are people-pleaser types, we waver between yes and no because we are afraid of disappointing people. But saying yes when we really want to say no is harmful to ourselves and our relationships. This habit can lead us into resentment and deceit. This week, practice saying no to things you really don't want to or can't do. Answer honestly with tact and grace, but don't feel obligated to explain why you're declining. If you do not have trouble saying no, you may want to adapt this practice to fit your context. Perhaps it would be important for you to focus energy on doing well the things you say yes to, or perhaps you need to practice saying yes to begin with. The goal for this practice is that people will know that you say what you mean and mean what you say.

Date(s) Used: _____

What did I learn about myself and/or God in this practice?

_____
_____
_____
_____
_____

Eighth Sunday after the Epiphany
Meditate on God's Glory

2 Corinthians 3:1-6

WE SO OFTEN credit ourselves with the work of freeing ourselves, changing ourselves, and finding our own new way, but it is God who does this for us. Time spent in God's presence transforms us; we don't need to try to make it happen. The more clearly we see God, the more clearly we will reflect God to others. This week, spend at least one hour giving attention to seeing God clearly. Meditation is the practice of focusing our attention on one thing for an extended period of time. You can think of it as a way to fix your gaze on God, without looking away. Use Psalm 19 to help you meditate on all that God is, and allow the words of the psalmist to sweep you into the wonder, mystery, and joy of being in God's presence. Take note of what happens within you when your focus is fixed on God.

Date(s) Used:_____

What did I learn about myself and/or God in this practice?

Transfiguration Sunday
Daily Prayer

Scripture: Mark 9:2-9

LIKE THE DISCIPLES, it can be hard for us to see God's presence and activity, even when it's right in front of us. This week, use these words as a daily prayer as we enter the season of Lent on Wednesday. Be open to nudges and prompts from the Spirit throughout each day as answers to your requests.

Oh Lord, bathe me in your presence.
My eyes are clouded; wash them so I can see you.
My ears are clogged; clean them out so I can hear you.
My heart is divided; heal me so I can love you.
And when I am able to see you, hear you, and love you well, grant me the courage to follow you wherever you lead.
Amen.

Date(s) Used: _____

What did I learn about myself and/or God in this practice?

_____
_____
_____
_____
_____
_____

THE SEASON OF LENT

On Transfiguration Sunday, the brilliance of God's revelation in Jesus turns the corner into a new kind of revelation found in the journey toward the cross. Ash Wednesday, the day we remember our humanity, begins our six-week observance of Lent. It is similar to Advent in that it is a season of preparation for what is to come. In these weeks, we walk with Jesus as he makes his way to the cross, taking on a whole new understanding of what it means to be Christ's disciples.

Most of us spend a lot of time and energy moving away from failure, and deep feeling, and fear—all of which are woven into the fabric of human existence. But in Lent we observe it, we sit with it, and we lament. It is the time we look with eyes wide open at who we really are and what the world is really like. This honest assessment drives home the reality that we need God, and it increases our desire for the things of God.

For most of its two-thousand-plus-year history, the church has observed Lent with fasting and prayer. We do not fast because it's a way to earn God's favor or get God's attention (it's neither); we fast because we want to become more aware of the things that keep us from following Jesus fully. In addition to the weekly practices suggested here, you may consider a particular item or activity from which you willingly choose to abstain throughout this season. Each Sunday in Lent is considered a "feast day," in anticipation of Easter that is to come, and the fasted items can be enjoyed on those days.

In this season of Lent, we take on practices to help us see ourselves and our world as we truly are. *And, as we do, may we also learn to see God for who God truly is: the God who loves us so much that God gives Godself away.*

First Sunday in Lent
Silence

Scripture: Mark 1:9-15

IT MAY SEEM strange to us that, between Jesus's baptism and the beginning of his ministry, he was led on a forty-day fast in the wilderness. Once again, we see Jesus doing things differently than we would. When we encounter struggle, we look for any part of the problem we can control and get to work. But Jesus went off into the wilderness in silence before saying anything at all. In silence, we find freedom from the need to control our surroundings, and we also find help to rely on God in the midst of struggle. This week, practice silence by choosing one half day or one whole day to be completely silent. Tell people ahead of time what to expect, and communicate through writing when necessary.

Date(s) Used: _____

What did I learn about myself and/or God in this practice?

Second Sunday in Lent
Honoring Others' Requests

Scripture: Mark 8:31-38

WHAT DOES IT look like to "take up our cross" to follow Jesus? While most of us will not be asked to give up our lives, the way of self-sacrifice is for all of us. This week, practice self-sacrifice in a small way by honoring the requests of others instead of doing things your way. As long as it does not harm yourself or another person, do what someone else prefers. If a request comes from a person you consider undeserving, remember you are not honoring the request for any other reason than obedience to Christ. Keep an open dialogue with Jesus about this, and notice what is happening within you with each request you honor. Requests come in all shapes and sizes, so make sure to include these common requests in your practice:

- Car with a blinker on asking to enter your lane
- Email asking a question, a favor, or a work order
- Voicemail or text asking for a call back
- Your children trying to get your attention
- The youth group kid asking for support of his mission trip
- A family member or spouse voicing concern or hurt

Date(s) Used:_____

What did I learn about myself and/or God in this practice?

Third Sunday in Lent
Recognizing our Sin

Scripture: John 2:13-22

JESUS'S ACTIONS IN the temple show a clear picture of God's wrath: decisive action against sin. Often, we assume that God's judgment is connected to the passionate and unpredictable anger we are accustomed to seeing in humans, but Jesus offers judgment as the way to healing and peace. This week, take some time in prayer to consider what Jesus may need to clean out of you. Are there any desires, activities, or decisions that are cluttering your life and preventing full worship? As they come to mind, write them down and offer them to Jesus. Allow him to clear out and burn away the things that are harmful to you. Receive his healing forgiveness, and listen for any other instructions. If you have recognized long patterns of behavior or addictions, ask Jesus to help you engage others in the process of healing.

Date(s) Used:_____

What did I learn about myself and/or God in this practice?

Fourth Sunday in Lent
Telling the Truth

Scripture: *John 3:14-21*

LYING IS ONE of the ways we hide from the light that exposes us. Of course, we don't usually call it lying; we call it fudging, or exaggerating, or maybe a white lie. This week, make it a practice to tell the truth in every circumstance. If someone asks if you've read such-and-such, don't pretend that you have. If you simply forget to call someone back, don't make up an excuse about why you didn't. When someone asks for your opinion, respond with tactful honesty, or decline to answer. If you find this practice difficult, use it as an opportunity to talk to Jesus about your tendency to lie. Ask him to help you see why this has become part of your habit of speech, and listen for his words of forgiveness, healing, and transformation.

Date(s) Used:_____

What did I learn about myself and/or God in this practice?

Fifth Sunday in Lent
Centering Prayer

Scripture: John 12:20-33

CHRISTIANS HAVE LONG practiced an ancient form of prayerful meditation known as *hesychasm*, contemplative prayer, centering prayer, or breath prayer. It is a simple practice of repeating a short prayer, scripture, or phrase to center ourselves in God's presence and create stillness in our minds. As we become grounded in the truth of the words, we become more aware of God's presence, and our desire to control our lives slowly subsides. This week, notice any time you feel frustrated or anxious—the telltale signs of losing control. Take this as your cue to practice centering prayer. Repeat your chosen phrase aloud or silently, following the rhythm of your breath, for as long as it takes to drown out the competing thoughts. Return to it as often as needed. Choose a phrase or short scripture that reminds you of truth, or you may want to use one of these as your centering prayer:

- Come, Lord Jesus (*inhale*); come (*exhale*).
- I was created from love (*inhale*), of love, and for love (*exhale*).
- Perfect love (*inhale*) drives out fear (*exhale*). (1 John 4:18)

Date(s) Used: _____

What did I learn about myself and/or God in this practice?

Palm Sunday/Sixth Sunday in Lent
Media Fast

Scripture: Mark 11:1-11

THIS WEEK, WE observe the final events of Jesus's life. We cannot fully celebrate the joy of resurrection unless we are willing to walk through death—both Jesus's death and our own dyings. We can make space and time for this journey by cutting out the many distractions that shout at us all the time. Media covers a wide range of things that surround us every day: television, radio, social media, music, electronic games and apps, even newspapers and magazines. If you are unable to fast from all of these items this week, fast from at least three sources of media that you use on a regular basis.

Date(s) Used:_____

What did I learn about myself and/or God in this practice?

THE SEASON OF EASTER

On Easter Sunday we celebrate God's promise of resurrection coming to life in the resurrected Christ—the future reality rushing into our present moment. But Easter is not something we can encapsulate in a single day. It requires a fifty-day season to probe, ponder, and practice the deep and wonderful mystery of resurrection.

The ancients referred to Easter as the eighth day of creation because, on Easter, God began the work of making all things new, beginning with resurrecting Christ from the dead. In Easter we hear God proclaim, "I am making everything new!" (Revelation 21:5), and we affirm that, indeed, "the old has gone, the new is here!" (2 Corinthians 5:17).

When we observe Easter as a season, we have time to experience that resurrection is God's new creation made real not just in Jesus but also in all of us who are in Christ. There is plenty of time to marvel in this good news because we aren't forced to cram it all in on one day. We are given time to notice where new life is springing up around us and inside of us. Easter is the season of learning how to live a new kind of life, called resurrection. *May you experience the joy, the freedom, and the excitement of new life in these days.*

Easter Sunday
Planting Seeds

Scripture: Mark 16:1-8

CHRIST'S RESURRECTION IS not just a singular event but a reality we are invited to participate in. This week, practice resurrection by planting seeds, whose growth from seed to blossom we cannot control yet is always a beautiful surprise. Plant them in a spot of good soil you will see often, and as they grow, be reminded to practice resurrection.

Date(s) Used: _____

What did I learn about myself and/or God in this practice?

Second Sunday of Easter
Seeking Sunlight

Scripture: 1 John 1:1–2:2

THIS WEEK, TAKE every opportunity to be in sunlight. Take a table by a window in a restaurant, walk outdoors, or take your lunch break on a park bench. As you enjoy the sunlight, be reminded that "God is light; in him there is no darkness at all" (1 John 1:5). Allow your imagination to wander on this theme, exploring all that it means for God to be all light and no darkness. Every time you search for sunlight this week, express your desire to live in the full light and life of God's presence.

Date(s) Used:_____

What did I learn about myself and/or God in this practice?

_____
_____
_____
_____
_____
_____
_____

Third Sunday of Easter
Driving the Speed Limit

Scripture: *1 John 3:1-7*

LIVING WITHOUT SIN is choosing obedience every time we're given the choice. But obedience is difficult for people of all ages because, if we're honest, we just don't want to submit to another person or authority. Submission doesn't mean we don't think for ourselves or lose our autonomy, but it does mean we suppress our own desire for control. This week, take simple steps of obedience by following the speed limit every time you drive. If you don't drive, take care to follow all posted signs for pedestrians and/or cyclists. When you find yourself speeding or jaywalking, let it serve as a reminder of your own difficulty with submission. Ask the Lord to help you trust him so that you *want* to submit to his authority.

Date(s) Used:_____

What did I learn about myself and/or God in this practice?

Fourth Sunday of Easter
Seeing Strangers as Siblings

Scripture: 1 John 3:16-24

ONE OF THE many gifts of resurrection life with God is our adoption into a very large and good family. This week, participate in this new world order of family that Christ has ushered in by seeing every person you encounter as your sibling. When it is appropriate, greet and talk to them as you would your brother or sister. When it is not appropriate, talk to God about them, praying for them as you might pray for a brother or sister. As you do this, notice what changes in you and what changes in your perception of the world. When you find this difficult, ask God to share with you his love for those you encounter.

Date(s) Used:_____

What did I learn about myself and/or God in this practice?

Fifth Sunday of Easter
Prepare for Sabbath

Scripture: John 15:1-8

SABBATH IS THE sacramental gift of time that allows us to rest in Jesus. We often forget that we are not required to produce the fruit but to stay close to the One who does. But, as good as it sounds, it can be really hard to practice a twenty-four-hour Sabbath in a culture so driven by activity and accomplishment. This week, practice *preparing* for Sabbath so that the day of rest can really be rest. Think ahead to what you would normally do on your Sabbath day—cleaning, buying groceries, cooking meals, making and/or keeping appointments, doing laundry—and do as much of it as you can ahead of time. You may also find that some tasks you normally do on that day can just wait to be done after your Sabbath. If you struggled with this practice during Advent, take this as another opportunity to receive this gift.

Date(s) Used: _____

What did I learn about myself and/or God in this practice?

Sixth Sunday of Easter
Love Feast

Scripture: John 15:9-17

AN ANCIENT TRADITION of the church is the Love Feast: a gathering of believers around good food, with no other purpose than to love and enjoy one another. This week, plan a Love Feast with some friends in your home, at your church, or at a favorite restaurant. It doesn't have to be fancy, but it does need to be done with intention. One of the ways we love one another is by sharing food, so invite each person to bring (or pay for) a favorite dish to share with the group. As you eat together, use the conversation to encourage one another. If this is a group that knows one another well, you may even invite people to share what they love about each person. Above all, enjoy!

Date(s) Used: _____

What did I learn about myself and/or God in this practice?

HOLY DAYS: ASCENSION, PENTECOST, TRINITY SUNDAY

On Pentecost Sunday, we love to tell and retell the story of the Holy Spirit coming to the disciples in the upper room. Ascension Sunday and Trinity Sunday, on the other hand, are lesser known and, frankly, just not as exciting. But the observance of each day shapes us further into the way of Jesus as we encounter mystery, power, and a reality beyond our comprehension or control.

Ascension Sunday is the final Sunday in the season of Easter, and it marks the day that Christ ascended into heaven. We are reminded that Jesus did not remain on earth to continue a limited human existence in one place at one time. Rather, he ascended into the heavenly realm, where his presence and authority extend throughout all time and space. Observing this day gives us opportunity to consider this mystery, even if it doesn't offer many answers.

After Jesus's ascension, he gave the disciples a command to pray and wait for the Holy Spirit, who would act as an advocate, teacher, and comforter. On Pentecost Sunday, we remember when the Holy Spirit did indeed come as an unexpected mighty wind and fire—tangible evidence of God's presence from Israel's earliest days. This event is what we celebrate as the birthday of the church, when the disciples were empowered to preach in all kinds of languages and thousands believed the gospel of Jesus Christ.

On Trinity Sunday, we explore yet another mystery that will carry us through the rest of the year. There is no one scripture that specifically teaches us the doctrine of the Trinity. But early in the church's existence, as they

ruminated on Jesus's teachings and their own experiences, Christians began to recognize the three persons of God as Father, Son, and Spirit.

During these weeks of pondering mystery and power, our practices help us remember that we are only recipients of God's miraculous works. *May we receive, and may we respond in obedience.*

Ascension Sunday/ Seventh Sunday of Easter
One Thing at a Time

Scripture: John 17:6-19

THIS WEEK, TRADE your accomplished multitasking abilities for doing only one thing at a time. Multitasking is certainly not sinful, but it can make it hard for us to focus on what's right in front of us. Jesus has prayed that we will be united, protected, filled with joy, and aware of the truth. Distraction and busyness have a way of working against each of these. If you usually make phone calls while you drive, just drive. If you usually scroll through social media as you watch a movie, do one or the other but not both. When you are with family or friends, give your full attention to your conversation. Enjoy the freedom of being undivided, and live in one moment, with one purpose at a time. You may even become aware that Jesus's prayers for you are being answered.

Date(s) Used:_____

What did I learn about myself and/or God in this practice?

Pentecost Sunday
Prayer Walk

Scripture: Ezekiel 37:1-14

THE BREATH OF God's Spirit brings life wherever it blows, and like Ezekiel, we are invited to participate in the process of bringing dead things to life. This week, set aside at least thirty minutes to walk around your own neighborhood or (if they are different) the neighborhood around your church. As you do, look for signs of life: new construction, babies and young children, schools, gardens, neighbors in conversation. Give thanks for the new life you see, and pray that the fullness of God's kingdom would flourish in each home, business, school, and conversation. Also keep your eyes open for signs of dry bones: abandoned buildings, empty sidewalks, overgrown lots, discarded trash/litter. Pray that the Spirit of God would breathe resurrection life into the people and systems represented. If one landmark stands out to you during your walk, make note of it, and return often to pray for life to flourish there.

Date(s) Used: _____

What did I learn about myself and/or God in this practice?

_____
_____
_____
_____
_____
_____

Trinity Sunday
Fly a Kite

Scripture: John 3:1-17

THE TRINITY—THE RELATIONSHIP of Father, Son, and Spirit—is mysterious and wonderful. It cannot fully be described or explained, but Jesus invites us to *experience* it. This week, take some time to fly a kite in the wind as a way to remember and experience the Spirit's activity in your life. If you can't fly a kite, look for another opportunity to experience the activity of the wind. Observe a flag being blown, or just stand still on a windy day. Use the time to ponder how you are being swept up into the activity of the triune God, and reflect on whether you are being moved by the wind or fighting against it.

Date(s) Used: _____

What did I learn about myself and/or God in this practice?

_____
_____
_____
_____
_____

YEAR B

ORDINARY TIME

It seems significant that Trinity Sunday is our entryway into the longest "non-season season" of the Christian calendar: Ordinary Time. Like the doctrine of the Trinity, which the church discovered through the ordinary ebbs and flows of life, so in Ordinary Time we learn to walk with Jesus in the days that go unmarked and unnamed.

The seasons of Advent, Christmas, Epiphany, Lent, and Easter heighten our awareness for what God is doing in the world, but the months in Ordinary Time can have a way of dulling our awareness. The summer and back-to-school months also bring disruptions to our schedules with travel and vacations, followed by a flurry of activity to get back into gear. If we are not careful, we can check out altogether until, suddenly, it's time for Advent again!

If we learn to pay attention, however, we will find that some of the most ordinary things are actually extraordinary things that we just get used to—because they happen all the time. The days grow longer and then shorter again as evidences of our planet's movement around the sun. Seeds—once just tiny bits buried in soil—grow into beautiful flowers, sweet fruit, and nourishing vegetables. Our playgrounds echo with the sounds of shrieks and laughter. Bike paths and lakes and sidewalks fill with people enjoying God's good creation. The wonders of Ordinary Time are all around us.

And in these wonders of Ordinary Time, we are invited into a new experience of our triune God at work. While the seasons invite us to walk through the story of Jesus, we now have opportunity to notice how Jesus is walking with us. We find freedom to explore the particular themes of our own journey as we discern the Spirit's guidance in the very ordinary activities of life.

The Lectionary offers scheduled texts for each Sunday in Ordinary Time, but the Ordinary Time practices in this book are organized by theme rather than scriptural text. Using the freedom and discernment of Ordinary Time, you can hop and skip around, choosing a pattern of practices that best fits your own journey through these weeks. Directly following the Ordinary Time section is one that contains practices designed for specific events that may occur during our observance of Ordinary Time, or at any other time throughout the year. These events and the practices for them include election day, vacation, and tragedy.

The practices of Ordinary Time are designed to help us partner with the Spirit in growing good fruit in ourselves. *May you be aware of God in all the ordinary places, and may you know comfort and peace as Jesus walks with you there.*

PRACTICING WITH SCRIPTURE

Scripture is a gift for us not only to learn about God but also to encounter God. We usually approach the Bible the way we approach a textbook or a newspaper, trying to understand information. This isn't wrong, but Scripture does more than inform us—it also forms us. The following nine practices can help us move beyond reading words to experiencing the transformational work of the Spirit through Scripture.

Practicing with Scripture
Memorize Scripture

FOR THOSE WHO grew up going to Sunday school or competing in Bible quizzing, there may be a lot of memorized Scripture stored away. But for many of us, memorization is a lost art in the age of the Bible app and search engines that can pull up chapter and verse, even with the vaguest of searches. Yet memorizing Scripture offers a gift beyond quick recall or a coveted Sunday school award. The process of memorization allows us to spend time with the words and their meaning so that they weave into our hearts, not just our minds. This week, practice memorizing 2 Peter 1:3. Write the verse and post it all throughout your home, car, and office. Read it each time you see it, until you can say it by memory. As you do, ask that the Spirit will help you experience the truth of the verse.

Ordinary Time

Date(s) Used: _____

What did I learn about myself and/or God in this practice?

_____

_____

_____

Practicing with Scripture
Read Jonah

THE STORY OF Jonah is both fascinating and challenging. This week, set aside thirty to sixty minutes to read the story of Jonah in its entirety. Enter into it as you would a novel or short work of fiction, noticing all the details and becoming absorbed in the story. After you've read it, prayerfully consider the following questions. You might want to journal and/or dialogue with others about your thoughts.

- Which characters exemplify righteousness in this story?
- What do you learn about God through this story?
- What does this story say about humans, especially God-fearing ones?
- What questions does this story raise for you?
- Why do you think this story is included in Scripture?
- With whom do you most identify in this story, and why?
- How is God challenging or encouraging you through Jonah's story?

Date(s) Used:_____

What did I learn about myself and/or God in this practice?

Practicing with Scripture
Being Made

THIS WEEK, SPEND time with a favorite passage of yours. If you don't have a favorite passage, use the widely popular Psalm 23. After reading, take time to ponder what this scripture is making or forming in you. Bring this question with you every time you read your scripture this week, paying close attention to the emotions, ideas, and memories that stir as you read. You may want to write down some of your thoughts and experiences as you notice what is being made or formed in you.

Date(s) Used: _____

What did I learn about myself and/or God in this practice?

_____

_____

_____

_____

_____

Ordinary Time

Practicing with Scripture
Lectio Divina

LATIN FOR "DIVINE reading," Lectio Divina is an ancient tool that invites the reader (or hearer) to read slowly with space to listen. We invite the Holy Spirit to use these ancient words to speak unique and personal words to us. Begin by using 1 Corinthians 13, and allow about thirty to forty-five minutes for this practice.

- Read the passage two times slowly, out loud if possible, with a few moments of silence in between. Listen for a word or phrase that sticks out to you, and make note of it.
- Read through a third time, pausing when you come to the word or phrase you wrote down.
- Put away the text, and ponder the word or phrase in silence. Turn it over in your mind, and see what memories or other scriptures come to mind.
- Ask the Spirit to help you understand what God wants to say to you in these words. Why is this important for you now?
- Rest in silence for a time.
- Respond and give thanks. What do you need to do with what you have heard? Give thanks for the way the Spirit has communicated to you.
- Record. Write down what you want to remember from this time.

Date(s) Used:_____

What did I learn about myself and/or God in this practice?

Practicing with Scripture
Praying the Psalms

THE PSALMS WERE the prayer and songbook of the Jewish people. They were sung, memorized, and prayed in synagogues, homes, and at the temple. Jesus used many of these words to form his own prayers, and we can use them to shape our prayers as well. Read Psalm 46 slowly, using each phrase to give language to your own conversation with God about the specifics in your life. If these words about God are true, we can use them to ask God to be true to God's character in our own situations. Consider these questions to guide you:

- When have you experienced God's help in times of trouble? (verse 1)
- What situations, past or present, make you feel like the mountains are crumbling or the oceans roaring? (verses 2–3)
- What wars do you need God to end? (verses 4–9)
- Ask God to help you be still now. (verse 10)
- When have you known God's presence in your midst? (verse 11)

Date(s) Used: _____

What did I learn about myself and/or God in this practice?

Practicing with Scripture
Contemplation of Scripture/Imaginative Prayer

CONTEMPLATION ALLOWS US to engage in conversation with Jesus as we imagine ourselves in the words of Scripture. Set aside at least thirty minutes for this practice as you follow this pattern:

- Begin by praying that the Holy Spirit leads your imagination through this practice.
- Read John 8:1–11 (or any story about Jesus) slowly at least two times.
- Imagine the scene and the characters of the story as if you were there yourself. Take time to enter into the experience of those who were present—either as the woman, a disciple, or a member of the crowd.
- What thoughts, emotions, or questions rise up in you? Imagine yourself there with Jesus, and talk to him about what you feel, think, or wonder.
- Ask Jesus to help you see things—including yourself/your character—as he does.
- Write down any insights you gain.

Date(s) Used:_____

What did I learn about myself and/or God in this practice?

Practicing with Scripture
One Chapter before Sleep

WHATEVER YOUR NORMAL bedtime routine is, swap it out this week for reading one chapter of the Bible before you fall asleep. Don't read to study or cram information. Instead, read to be reminded of God's goodness and presence. If you are too tired to finish the whole chapter, that's okay. If you're not tired and you read more than one chapter, that's okay too! Allow the words you've read to keep you company as you drift off to sleep. At the end of the week, notice whether this practice has affected your sleep patterns or dreams at all.

Date(s) Used: _____

What did I learn about myself and/or God in this practice?

_____
_____
_____
_____
_____

Ordinary Time

Practicing with Scripture
Read the Gospel of John

WHEN WE READ with formation in mind, we usually zone in on small portions of Scripture at a time. But this week, read through the entire book of John, just like you would read any other book or story. Start at the beginning, reading as often as you can, for as long as you are able at a time. Reading from start to finish allows us to see the big picture, noticing themes and connections we often miss when we read in smaller segments. Read with expectation and wonder, allowing the story of Jesus to capture your imagination and bring you in. When you have finished John, take time to consider and/or write down your reflections. How did you encounter Jesus in John's writing? What did you see new or fresh reading it this way? Is there a particular message that left an impression on you while you read?

Date(s) Used: _____

What did I learn about myself and/or God in this practice?

Practicing with Scripture
Meditate

IN DESCRIBING THE profound, self-emptying humility of Christ, the apostle Paul preserved an ancient, beautiful hymn of the church. This week, reserve twenty to thirty minutes to meditate on the mystery described in Philippians 2:6–11. In meditation, we give time to consider deeper levels of thought, understanding, and experience. When we meditate on Scripture, we do not seek so much to figure out the mystery as we do to explore and experience the mystery. Do not be surprised if this practice leaves you with more questions than answers. Rejoice in the magnitude of a God who is greater than we can comprehend!

Date(s) Used:_____

What did I learn about myself and/or God in this practice?

NURTURING THE FRUIT OF THE SPIRIT

It is the Spirit's work to grow good fruit in us, but we can engage in practices that either encourage or hinder that work. Use the next seventeen practices to partner with God as the Spirit grows good, beautiful fruit in you.

Love, Joy, and Peace
Gratitude

THE PRACTICE OF being grateful for what we have is the greatest antidote to greed and our culture's insatiable need for more. Gratitude is also inextricably linked to joy. When we take time to be grateful, we cultivate joy deep within ourselves. This week, practice gratitude in one of these ways:

- Set aside five minutes each day to recall one good gift you've been given and think on all that it has done for you. It may be a conversation with a friend, a thoughtful note, or even a meaningful experience with Scripture.
- Look for at least five things each day you are grateful for, and create a running list for the week.
- Choose one day to write as many thank-you notes as you can, to anyone who comes to mind.

Date(s) Used: _____

What did I learn about myself and/or God in this practice?

Love, Joy, and Peace
Awareness of God in Creation

CHOOSE AT LEAST one day this week during which you will allow yourself time to become deeply absorbed in nature as a way of experiencing God's goodness. Instead of rushing past your ordinary landscape, take some time to notice the extraordinary in it. Pay great attention to the sights, sounds, and colors of nature, and marvel in their beauty. As you sit in creation, give your attention to enjoying it as you would a famous painting in an art museum. God, the Master Artist, has put all of creation before us to bring forth joy and beauty. Know that, even if it looks like you are doing nothing, you are engaged in holy work.

Date(s) Used:_____

What did I learn about myself and/or God in this practice?

_____

_____

_____

_____

_____

Ordinary Time

Love, Joy, and Peace
Turning from Worry

"Do not be anxious about anything, but in every situation, by prayer and petition, with thanksgiving, present your requests to God. And the peace of God, which transcends all understanding, will guard your hearts and your minds in Christ Jesus."

—Philippians 4:6–7

THIS WEEK, PRACTICE replacing worry with prayer. Notice your concern, fear, and worry every time they appear, but do not immediately shut them off. Instead, turn them into specific requests; then release them to God. Relax into the peace of Christ guarding you, and keep on the lookout for answered prayers. If you need a tangible reminder to turn your mind from worry to prayer, consider putting an object in your pocket, like a coin, a paper clip, or perhaps a small cross. Each time you find yourself worrying, put your hand in your pocket to feel for the object and turn your mind to prayer.

Date(s) Used:_____

What did I learn about myself and/or God in this practice?

Love, Joy, and Peace
Sleep

OUR SPIRITS, MINDS, and bodies need sleep to function well. Sleep is a gift, but many of us avoid it or have trouble yielding to it. In a very real way, sleep is an act of faith: we can rest because we know that God is at work even while we sleep, and God is with us even when we are alone in the silence. And we know that God made us to rest because God made us in his image, and God himself rested after the work of creation. This week, practice sleep by doing one of the following:

- Choose one day to sleep until you cannot sleep any longer.
- Choose three nights on which you will plan to sleep one hour longer than usual.
- Take a nap during the day, on as many days as possible.

Date(s) Used: _____

What did I learn about myself and/or God in this practice?

Ordinary Time

Love, Joy, and Peace
Pray for Justice

"But let justice roll on like a river, righteousness like a never-failing stream!"
—Amos 5:24

USE THIS VERSE as a guide for prayer every time you see or hear about injustice this week—whether you're driving, reading the news, or talking to a family member. You may choose to write this verse down and post it where you can see it often as a reminder to pray. When confronted with injustice, take a few minutes to pray for the individuals involved, asking the Lord to make things right. After you pray, don't be surprised if God directs you to do or say something on behalf of the person being treated unjustly. Be open to ways God wants to use you to answer your own prayers.

Date(s) Used:_____

What did I learn about myself and/or God in this practice?

Love, Joy, and Peace
Journaling

MUCH OF WHAT we now have as Scripture began as spiritual memoir: personal stories recorded by individuals who encountered God. Throughout human history, people have made the practice of writing part of their spiritual formation. When we write, it can become clear to us where God is working in our lives and what God's activity looks like. This week, grab a notebook and spend fifteen minutes reflecting on the events of your day or on what you have read in Scripture. Don't worry about spelling words right, good handwriting, or watching what you say. Write prayerfully and honestly. At the end of the week, take time to read back over what you have written and look for evidences of God's presence and activity.

Date(s) Used: _____

What did I learn about myself and/or God in this practice?

_____
_____
_____
_____
_____

Ordinary Time

Patience, Kindness, and Goodness
Take a Resonate Walk

THIS WEEK, PLAN for an hour-long walk in an area of the city you are connected to in some way, whether it's where you live, near your work, surrounding your church, or a place you walk or drive by frequently. As you walk, look and listen for people, things, sights, and smells that resonate with you. Make an effort to be aware and observant. You're not walking to get somewhere; you're walking to learn or feel something. Don't be afraid to greet or ask questions of those you encounter, and listen for their answers. Throughout your walk use this prayer to help you resonate with God's heart for this area: *"God, help me to think your thoughts and feel your feelings for the people and places I see."* After the hour is up, take a few minutes to reflect on and/or journal your experience. How did God answer your prayer? Are you being invited to do anything as a result?

Date(s) Used:_____

What did I learn about myself and/or God in this practice?

Patience, Kindness, and Goodness
Encourage a Kid

YOU DON'T HAVE to be a parent to help raise a kid. Children and teenagers thrive when they feel valued and known by the adults who surround them. This week, go out of your way to let a child or teen know you value them. Send a card, give a gift, or ask their parents if you can take them out for ice cream. It may be a niece, nephew, neighbor, a coworker's child, or someone in your church. If you're having trouble identifying a child to encourage this week, pray about it and see how the Lord leads you. If you *are* a child or teen, think about an adult who makes you feel welcome and valued. Find a way to tell them how much they mean to you this week.

Date(s) Used:_____

What did I learn about myself and/or God in this practice?

Ordinary Time

Patience, Kindness, and Goodness
Invite a Neighbor

THIS WEEK, INVITE one of your neighbors to your home, porch, or backyard for a meal. There is no agenda other than getting to know one another better and extending the gift of hospitality. You don't have to prepare a fancy meal or have an immaculately clean house. Focus your attention on being a good neighbor by expressing care, listening to stories, and sharing what you have. If you find yourself needing to do something more spiritual than just eat together, remember that Jesus tells us loving our neighbor is spiritual. It is one of the ways we worship God.

Date(s) Used:_____

What did I learn about myself and/or God in this practice?

Patience, Kindness, and Goodness
Microwave Prayers

OUR LIVES HAVE been conditioned by fast food, high-speed internet, microwavable meals, and two-day shipping. We assume that anything worth having can and should come to us right away. But this is not the way we see God work, nor is it the way that is best for us. Every time you use the microwave this week, acknowledge the ways you are shaped to expect immediate results. While your food is heating up, use the time to ask God to help you grow into faithful, patient obedience, regardless of whether you see the fruit of your obedience right away.

Date(s) Used: _____

What did I learn about myself and/or God in this practice?

_____
_____
_____
_____
_____
_____

Ordinary Time

Patience, Kindness, and Goodness
Intercession

GOD INVITES US to partner with him in his work; sometimes it is through actions, but it's always through prayer. This week, practice intercession, which is praying for the good of another person. Follow these guidelines as you pray this week:

- If you do not immediately know whom you should pray for, ask God to give you a name. Spend a few moments in silence to hear it.
- Ask what God's desires are for this person. Be aware that it might be different than what you desire. Again, take time to listen in silence.
- Pray as Jesus taught us: for God's desire and God's kingdom to come in this person's life.
- Continue to pray for this person all week, maybe even setting aside a particular time each day to pray for her or him.
- Ask the Lord if he wants you to share with this person how you have been praying for her or him. If so, write your prayer in a note. If not, continue praying in secret.

Date(s) Used: _____

What did I learn about myself and/or God in this practice?

Faithfulness, Gentleness, and Self-Control
Suspending Judgment

IT CAN BE very easy to assess another person's wrongdoing from afar and assume we know the best way to fix it. But Jesus says good fruit and a good foundation come from using his words in our *own* lives, not getting others to use his words in *their* lives. This week, pay attention to the often-subtle process of judging others in your thoughts, whether you say them aloud or not. Each time this happens, suspend the process of judging another person's actions, demeanor, behavior, or decisions. Then ask the Holy Spirit to help you see the places in your own life where you need to listen to and obey the words of Jesus.

Date(s) Used:_____

What did I learn about myself and/or God in this practice?

Faithfulness, Gentleness, and Self-Control
Learning from Mary

"Mary responded, 'Oh, how my soul praises the Lord. How my spirit rejoices in God my Savior! For he took notice of his lowly servant girl, and from now on all generations will call me blessed.'"

—Luke 1:46–48, NLT

MARY—THE TEENAGE, UNWED, illiterate mother of Jesus—exhibited tremendous courage in accepting God's call on her life. This week, take time to reflect on her words of celebration. She risked her reputation, her well-being, her own dreams, and her entire future; yet her response is one of joy and not fear. What might the Spirit want to say to you through Mary's courageous, faithful action?

Date(s) Used:_____

What did I learn about myself and/or God in this practice?

Faithfulness, Gentleness, and Self-Control
Change Your Morning Ritual

THE MORNING RITUAL for many of us includes rotating through various apps on our phones shortly after we wake. This week, exchange your technology-centered morning ritual for one of stillness. Instead of looking at your phone right away each morning, try something new this week, like getting out of bed as soon as your alarm goes off and making the bed immediately. Or try going to a different room (without your phone) and sitting in silence for a few minutes. Whatever you choose, develop a new ritual of your own that imprints you with the desire to seek God's presence instead of distraction.

Date(s) Used: _____

What did I learn about myself and/or God in this practice?

_____
_____
_____
_____
_____
_____

Ordinary Time

Faithfulness, Gentleness, and Self-Control
Fasting

WE DO NOT fast in order to get God's attention or earn credit with him but to focus our own hearts as we pray. Practice fasting this week, and as you do so, ask the Holy Spirit to give you a desire for God that is greater than your desire for the food from which you are fasting. During times you would normally be eating, pray for a pressing need in your own life or in the life of someone you know. Choose one of these ways to fast this week:

- Fast one meal each day.
- Fast for one twenty-four-hour period during the week.
- Fast from a food that is a regular in your diet (e.g., coffee, bread, meat, etc.).

Date(s) Used: _____

What did I learn about myself and/or God in this practice?

Faithfulness, Gentleness, and Self-Control
Seek Out a Mentor

EACH OF US needs the encouragement and wisdom of a mentor, someone who has walked the way of Jesus a little longer than we have. This week, ask God to guide you to a mentor or to recognize the mentor(s) you already have. Whom do you know that is living the way you want to live? Who speaks godly words into your life? If someone is already acting as a mentor for you, let them know that this week. Thank them for their role in your life. If not, consider whom you want to learn from, and look for ways to spend time together in conversation and prayer.

Date(s) Used:_____

What did I learn about myself and/or God in this practice?

Ordinary Time

Faithfulness, Gentleness, and Self-Control
A Day without Spending

THOSE OF US who can buy things whenever we want tend to forget that we often already have what we need. Our ability to spend can get in the way of remembering God's abundance and make us think we are the ones providing for ourselves. This week, choose one day to go without making any purchases. Make your lunch instead of buying it. Plan to fill your tank with gas on another day. Avoid the vending machine, the shopping mall, and your Amazon app. As you do this, pray for those who cannot spend freely, and thank the God who provides for our needs out of his abundance.

Date(s) Used: _____

What did I learn about myself and/or God in this practice?

_____
_____
_____
_____
_____
_____

PRACTICES FOR NOT-SO-ORDINARY TIME: VACATION, ELECTIONS, TRAGEDY

In the midst of Ordinary Time there are often weeks that feel anything but ordinary. Vacation is a planned escape from the ordinary, while tragic events come unexpectedly and uproot all sense of normalcy. And, for those who follow the news closely, election season often has a life all its own. Find these practices when you need them, and use them to connect you to the God who is unchanging but certainly not ordinary.

A Practice for Vacation
Laugh

WE SAY LAUGHTER is the best medicine, but we usually don't think of it as being very holy. Joy is actually one of God's best gifts, and laughter is an expression of this holy gift. This week, look for every opportunity to laugh. Tell and listen for jokes, watch your favorite sitcom, look for the humor in every situation. Laughter is infectious and healing, so include as many people as you can.

Date(s) Used:_____

What did I learn about myself and/or God in this practice?

A Practice for Election Season
Pray for a Competitor

THE POLITICAL RHETORIC of our culture is often divisive, dehumanizing, and even violent. We never hear politicians inviting us to love, bless, or pray for their opponents—but Jesus does invite us to that practice. On this election day, pray for the candidate you are *not* voting for, and pray also for all those who are voting for that candidate. You are not praying that the candidate will change, or that they will lose. Instead, practice loving them by praying that God shines his full goodness, mercy, love, and joy on them. Remember that each of these individuals is dearly loved by God, just as you are. Pray that they would know this truth.

Date(s) Used: _____

What did I learn about myself and/or God in this practice?

_____
_____
_____
_____
_____
_____

Not-so-Ordinary Time

A Practice during Tragedy
Lament

WHEN TERRIBLE THINGS happen, there is often no better response than to cry. Even Jesus wept outside his dead friend's tomb. This week, allow yourself to do the holy work of lament. Lament is uninhibited grief over what is not as it should be. Whenever you encounter or remember injustice, brokenness, pain, suffering, or rejection this week, know that Jesus laments these things too. Ask Jesus to share his feelings with you as you join in his love for his people.

Date(s) Used: _____

What did I learn about myself and/or God in this practice?

CHRIST THE KING SUNDAY

Christ the King Sunday is the final Sunday of Ordinary Time, before the church year begins anew with Advent. Once again, we will grow in hopeful anticipation as we learn to wait in the dark. But if we're not careful, we could be fooled into thinking that all we have to hope for and expect is the presents, the decadent food, or the glittering decorations of our Christmas celebrations.

Christ the King Sunday offers us a clear picture of what we expectantly await during Advent—our King and his kingdom to come on earth, even as it is in heaven. We are reminded that our King is unlike any other king, and his kingdom unlike any other kingdom. So we should not be surprised if we find ourselves becoming unlike other people.

In this week before Advent, we enter a kind of preparation before the preparation. *Let us fix our eyes on King Jesus, and may we find our home in his kingdom.*

Christ the King Sunday
Meditate on the Kingdom

Scripture: John 18:33-37

MEDITATION IS THE practice of focusing our attention on one thing for an extended period of time. It is especially helpful to meditate on things that seem paradoxical or confusing at first. Jesus says many things that are not immediately easy to understand, but he also invites us to ponder his words further. This week, set aside at least thirty minutes, perhaps using your normal time for Bible reading and prayer, to meditate on Christ's kingdom. What is it? Where is it? What does it mean that Jesus's kingdom is "not of this world"? As you ponder these questions, ask the Spirit to guide you not only to understand but also to experience the kingdom of Christ.

Date(s) Used:_____

What did I learn about myself and/or God in this practice?

YEAR C

THE SEASON OF ADVENT

We often assume Advent is the countdown to Christmas: the church equivalent of how many shopping days we have left. The season does begin four Sundays prior to Christmas Day, but we aren't preparing ourselves for Christ coming as a baby. Instead, Advent is the preparation of people who live in the in-between: looking back on Christ's birth, and looking forward to when Christ will come again.

As a result, the scriptures of Advent feel decidedly un-Christmasy. They are filled with prophetic words of judgment against oppressive earthly powers and proclamations of the justice and peace that will replace these powers in God's kingdom. Advent is not so much a season of light and hope as a season of waiting in the dark.

It is significant that the Christian calendar begins this way. We begin the year in an honest place, admitting that we do, in fact, need saving, and that the One who saves chooses to do it in a different way than we expect.

In these weeks, we do not celebrate the God who comes to us on *our* schedule, conforming to *our* list of requirements. In Advent, we recognize that God comes to us not in the way or timeline we *expect* but in the way we *need*. The best things—forming new life, making people whole, restoring the world—cannot be rushed.

During this season, we will take on practices that help us prepare our hearts and minds for this God who comes to us. *May we grow in awareness, trust, and expectation of our God as we wait in the dark.*

First Sunday of Advent
Worship

Scripture: Luke 21:25-36

ADVENT IS A season of hopeful anticipation, but if we are not careful, the weeks before Christmas can become a season of frantic, anxious activity. Worship sets our hearts and minds on what is really happening in this season and what we anticipate in Christ's coming. This is something that can be practiced throughout the week—you don't need to wait for Sunday! Look for every opportunity to focus your attention and desire on the God who comes to us, bursting through the door with hope. Ask and expect that God will expand your hopeful imagination as you worship. These can all be practices of worship:

- Spend at least ten minutes a day with an Advent Scripture guide of your choice, or use the Revised Common Lectionary Advent scriptures for Year C.
- Whenever possible, listen to music that inspires your heart to sing for joy.
- Read and reread stories of hope, joy, and love.

Date(s) Used:_____

What did I learn about myself and/or God in this practice?

Second Sunday of Advent
Share Hope

Scripture: Luke 3:1-6

IT SEEMS WE are surrounded by bad news all the time. Stories of war, disease, deceit, violence, and oppression come to us in a twenty-four-hour news cycle on every media platform. It can be easy to despair, but God's activity is breaking in, even in the worst of circumstances. Like John the Baptist, whose ministry began in a dark time under a lineup of evil and oppressive leaders, we too carry a message of hope: things will not always be this way! This week, look for every opportunity to offer hope in your daily conversations and tasks. Hope isn't shallow; it is not merely offering cheery words or turning a blind eye to pain. It is a persistent belief that God is doing good work on our behalf, even when we can't see it. When you encounter particularly difficult situations this week, first ask God to show you how to hope; then ask him to help you share hope with others.

Date(s) Used: _____

What did I learn about myself and/or God in this practice?

_____
_____
_____
_____
_____
_____

Third Sunday of Advent
Give without Expectation

Scripture: Luke 3:7-18

IN THIS SEASON of gift-buying and gift-giving, most of the people on our list are those who also have us on their lists. This week, take time to consider someone to whom you can give a gift without any expectation of receiving one in return. Ask the Lord to give you eyes to see those he wants to bless through you. If it's hard to think of someone, consider one of these options:

- Purchase some items on the wish list for a local charitable organization.
- Find out what a single mom needs for her kids this Christmas.
- Bless a barista or server with a generous tip.
- Buy and wrap something special for the coworker who is without family.

Date(s) Used: _____

What did I learn about myself and/or God in this practice?

Advent

Fourth Sunday of Advent
Give Your Presence

Scripture: Luke 1:39-45

CHRISTMAS IS OUR celebration of the incarnation: Jesus giving himself to us. And it has come to us through Mary, who gave herself fully to God. To remember and share the fullness of Jesus's gift this week, we will practice giving more—not necessarily more presents but more of *ourselves*. As you spend time with family and friends this week, think about your time, your conversation, and the way you listen as gifts you give. Look for every opportunity to communicate "I love you"—whether by saying those words, by your actions, or both. Giving of ourselves in this way requires us to be fully present. It's very personal, and it can be risky. But as we engage in this small practice of incarnation, the fullness of God's gift can come alive in us. And we may find that we are giving the gift our friends and families want most from us!

Date(s) Used: _____

What did I learn about myself and/or God in this practice?

THE TWELVE DAYS OF CHRISTMAS

For most American Evangelical Christians, what we know of the twelve days of Christmas is from a song—of which the only words we all know for sure are "FIVE GOLDEN RINGS!" But for most of the history of the church, Christmas has been celebrated for twelve full days, from December 25 through January 5. This short season ends with the commemoration of the Epiphany of the Magi on January 6, which ushers in the much longer season of Epiphany.

During the twelve days of Christmas, we take time to appreciate the wonder of the incarnation: God who comes to dwell with us, becoming like us. It is a season decidedly opposed to the consumer mentality that engulfs a typical American Christmas celebration. Christ is not just one of the gifts we unwrap in a hurry and forget about a few days later. These days give us time to savor, enjoy, and bask in the goodness that is God-with-us.

Christmas Day and Epiphany are always the same dates: December 25 and January 6. Because these dates fall on different days of the week each year, there may not always be two Sundays within the twelve days of Christmas. The Sunday on or immediately following January 6 is celebrated as Epiphany Sunday.

May these days of Christmas be full of joy as we receive the God who comes to us.

Christmas Day or First Sunday after Christmas
Praying the Daily Examen

Scripture: Luke 2:41-52

EVEN AS A child, Jesus was keenly aware of his Father's presence, and joined in his Father's work. St. Ignatius taught the Daily Examen as a way of praying in order to recognize God's presence and activity in our lives as well. We look back on the previous day, rummaging through our normal activities, to find where God has been with us. Over time with this practice, we learn to notice God in the way he comes to us, which is often much different than the way we expect him to come. To practice the Examen this week, set aside three to five minutes at the same time every day. It may be helpful to use a journal to jot down your observations as you pray.

1. Ask the Holy Spirit to help you see the last twenty-four hours as God sees them.
2. Focus on the day's gifts and give thanks for them.
3. What invitations or opportunities did God give you? Notice any moments of strong emotion as clues to God's activity and your response.
4. Ask the Spirit to guide you to one particular event or emotion of the day that is important, and pray repentance, gratitude, or a request/petition accordingly.
5. As you look toward the next day, ask specifically for what you need.

Date(s) Used: _____

What did I learn about myself and/or God in this practice?

Second Sunday after Christmas or Epiphany Sunday
Gratitude List

Scripture: Isaiah 60:1-6

IN THE BUSYNESS of the holiday season, it can be difficult to slow down to take stock of all we have been given. Yet when we receive gifts without practicing gratitude, we miss the whole point of the gifts in the first place. This week, clear some space for a practice of gratitude each day. Make a running list of things you are grateful for: things you have been given both spiritually and materially, people you know, experiences you've had—whatever you determine is a good gift in your life. See if you can list one hundred things before the week is over, but don't be surprised if you go over. You might find that, once you start, it's hard to stop!

Date(s) Used:_____

What did I learn about myself and/or God in this practice?

THE SEASON OF EPIPHANY

Epiphany may be the season least familiar to those of us in Protestant-Evangelical traditions. Yet it might be the most wonderful season of them all, filled with light, and joy, and pure astonishment at the wonder of God.

An epiphany is defined as "an appearance or manifestation, especially of a divine being," which is an apt description of what happened when Magi from the East discovered a star that told of a newborn king. But the story of the Magi is not just about their epiphany; it's an epiphany for us too. It reminds us that God is in the business of telling people about himself, even—and maybe especially—the people we assume don't know the first thing about God. During this season we revel in the light that God shines so that any and all can see God's glory. And, like the Magi, as we encounter the dazzling beauty of this God of light, love, and power, we find that we are changed.

Epiphany begins at the same time every year but has varying lengths depending on the date of Easter. The final Sunday in Epiphany is Transfiguration Sunday. Ash Wednesday, which marks the beginning of the season of Lent, falls in the week after Transfiguration Sunday. The date of Ash Wednesday is determined by counting back six weeks from the date of Easter. For each Lectionary year (Year A, Year B, Year C), this book includes the maximum amount of potential weeks for an Epiphany season, but most years will have fewer. Transfiguration Sunday will always be the Sunday directly preceding Ash Wednesday.

During Epiphany, we will engage in practices to help us receive the light God gives us. *May we be astonished and overjoyed—both by God's dazzling light and by what God's light grows in us.*

First Sunday after the Epiphany/ Baptism of the Lord
Letting Ourselves Be Loved

Scripture: Luke 3:15-17, 21-22

VERY OFTEN WHEN we come to God, we try to control the time and the conversation. This week, practice letting yourself be loved, letting yourself be given to, and letting yourself be acted upon by our good God. Set a time in which you can sit in silence for five minutes a day, or choose one day this week to sit in silence for thirty minutes. Focus your attention on receiving God's love and on letting God do or say whatever God wants. Pay attention to what images, memories, or emotions come to mind. After your time of silence, you may want to record your experience.

Date(s) Used: _____

What did I learn about myself and/or God in this practice?

Second Sunday after the Epiphany
Taste and See

Scripture: John 2:1-11

WE ARE INVITED to "taste and see that the Lord is good" (Psalm 34:8). This leads us into the delight, pleasure, and unbridled joy of God's new creation—like water being turned into really good wine. We are not only invited to work with God but also to celebrate with God in the anticipation of what is to come, and to enjoy what has already been given. This week, spend time doing something that brings you the full body, mind, and soul experience of pleasure. It might be a really good meal, your favorite dessert, a bubble bath, a stroll through the art museum, a favorite album, or unhurried conversation with a good friend. Whatever you choose, don't be shy about enjoying it. Celebrate the good in it! When you do, you won't even have to try to give thanks; gratitude is a natural response to true celebration.

Date(s) Used:_____

What did I learn about myself and/or God in this practice?

Third Sunday after the Epiphany
Spend Time among the Poor

Scripture: Luke 4:14-21

WE LOVE THE words of Isaiah 61, and we love that Jesus says he is their fulfillment: good news for the poor, captives set free, the blind able to see. But for many of us who are *not* poor or imprisoned, it can be hard to identify just what those actions might look like today. What *is* good news for the poor? How *do* the oppressed get free? This week, go out of your way to spend time among those who know what it means to be poor or oppressed. If you're not sure where to go, consider a homeless shelter, the courthouse or county jail, a recovery ministry, or a restaurant or hangout on the "other side" of town. If you know someone connected to one of these communities, ask that person to be your guide. While there, remember that your task is not to fix anyone but to learn from your neighbors. What does good news look like for them? How would they experience freedom, or how are they experiencing freedom? Invite Jesus to make his words come alive in new ways in you.

Date(s) Used:_____

What did I learn about myself and/or God in this practice?

Fourth Sunday after the Epiphany
Let It Go

Scripture: Luke 4:21-30

IT IS PUZZLING to us that Jesus did not even try to convince the people of his hometown that he was right. Even at the direst moment, when they were about to kill him, he just passed right through the crowd without a word, continuing on his way. This week, take your cue from Jesus and let go of your desire to convince others of your opinions. Whenever someone takes offense at your words or disagrees with your actions, resist the urge to explain yourself or to persuade them of your viewpoint. Hear the person out, and be open to change if it is needed. If you are confident you are in the right, continue on your way without taking their opinions with you. Ask Jesus to grant perspective and wisdom to know which action is needed in each situation.

Date(s) Used:_____

What did I learn about myself and/or God in this practice?

Fifth Sunday after the Epiphany
Into the Deep Waters

Scripture: Luke 5:1-11

JESUS TAUGHT THE crowds from the shallow end of the lake, but the deep water is the place of the true miracle—and the very personal conversation between Jesus and Peter. This week, venture out into the deep water with God. If you have access to a swimming pool or a body of water, literally swim or take a boat out to the deepest part. If not, look at a picture or recall an experience with deep water. Think about the risk, the possibility, and the mystery of those places. What is the deep water of your own self? What would it be like to go there with Jesus? Allow this time of pondering to lead you into a conversational prayer with Jesus. Say whatever you want to say, and listen for whatever Jesus wants to say to you.

Date(s) Used: _____

What did I learn about myself and/or God in this practice?

_____
_____
_____
_____
_____
_____
_____

Sixth Sunday after the Epiphany
Exegeting Advertisements

Scripture: Luke 6:17-26

PREACHERS, TEACHERS, AND scholars are taught the elements of exegesis: careful analysis of the biblical text using historical, literary, and theological lenses in order to uncover a faithful meaning from the text. This week, practice using the same methods to find the meaning in advertisements that we see and hear everywhere. As you engage in this process, ask Jesus to help you see the truth of his kingdom clearly. Each time you see, hear, or read an advertisement this week, pause long enough to ask yourself or those around you these questions:

- According to this message, what does it mean to be blessed?
- Who is to be avoided or pitied (the unblessed)?
- Who is the intended recipient of this message?
- How does this message recommend that you achieve the blessedness defined by the ad?
- How does this message affirm or contradict the blessings and sorrows of God's kingdom as described by Jesus?

Date(s) Used: _____

What did I learn about myself and/or God in this practice?

_____
_____
_____
_____
_____
_____

Seventh Sunday after the Epiphany
Praying for a Competitor

Scripture: Luke 6:27-38

MOST OF US would be hesitant to name anyone as our *enemy*. We know better than that. This week, practice praying for those you find yourself at odds with or recognize as competitors. At the beginning of the week, take some time to think of persons who make life difficult for you. It may be an estranged family member, a coworker, or an employee of a competing company. Post a list of these names somewhere you will see often, and pray for them each time you see it. You are not praying that these people will change. Instead, practice loving them by praying that God shines his full goodness, mercy, love, and joy on them. Remember that each of these individuals is dearly loved by God, just as you are. Pray that they would know this truth.

Date(s) Used: _____

What did I learn about myself and/or God in this practice?

_____
_____
_____
_____
_____
_____
_____

Epiphany

Eighth Sunday after the Epiphany
Suspending Judgment

Scripture: Luke 6:39-49

IT CAN BE very easy to assess another person's wrongdoing from afar and assume we know the best way to fix it. But Jesus says good fruit and a good foundation come from using his words in our *own* lives, not getting others to use his words in *their* lives. This week, pay attention to the often-subtle process of judging others in your thoughts, whether you say them aloud or not. Each time this happens, suspend the process of judging another person's actions, demeanor, behavior, or decisions. Then ask the Holy Spirit to help you see the places in your own life where you need to listen to and obey the words of Jesus.

Date(s) Used: _____

What did I learn about myself and/or God in this practice?

Transfiguration Sunday
Confession

Scripture: Luke 9:28–43a

TO PREPARE FOR our Lenten journey with Jesus to the cross, we will take on the practice of confession this week. Confession is simply telling the truth—agreeing with God about what God sees in us. Choose thirty minutes to walk through these prompts prayerfully, listening for the Spirit's direction. Participating in an Ash Wednesday service will be a helpful part of this week's practice as well.

- Ask to be reminded of God's love for you. Settle into the safety of our good God who can be trusted.
- Ask the Holy Spirit to shed light on something sinful that is keeping you from embracing God's work in your life.
- Remember that, while you may feel sad or uncomfortable, the voice of God never speaks in shaming language.
- Write down what comes to mind and the specific instances attached (for example, "I confess that I keep myself too busy to listen to God.")
- Finally, ask God to forgive you, heal you, and provide what you need to fully embrace God's work in your life.

Date(s) Used: _____

What did I learn about myself and/or God in this practice?

_____
_____
_____
_____
_____

Epiphany

THE SEASON OF LENT

On Transfiguration Sunday, the brilliance of God's revelation in Jesus turns the corner into a new kind of revelation found in the journey toward the cross. Ash Wednesday, the day we remember our humanity, begins our six-week observance of Lent. It is similar to Advent in that it is a season of preparation for what is to come. In these weeks, we walk with Jesus as he makes his way to the cross, taking on a whole new understanding of what it means to be Christ's disciples.

Most of us spend a lot of time and energy moving away from failure, and deep feeling, and fear—all of which are woven into the fabric of human existence. But in Lent we observe it, we sit with it, and we lament. It is the time we look with eyes wide open at who we really are and what the world is really like. This honest assessment drives home the reality that we need God, and it increases our desire for the things of God.

For most of its two-thousand-plus-year history, the church has observed Lent with fasting and prayer. We do not fast because it's a way to earn God's favor or get God's attention (it's neither); we fast because we want to become more aware of the things that keep us from following Jesus fully. In addition to the weekly practices suggested here, you may consider a particular item or activity from which you willingly choose to abstain throughout this season. Each Sunday in Lent is considered a "feast day," in anticipation of Easter that is to come, and the fasted items can be enjoyed on those days.

In this season of Lent, we take on practices to help us see ourselves and our world as we truly are. *And, as we do, may we also learn to see God for who God truly is: the God who loves us so much that God gives Godself away.*

First Sunday in Lent
Solitude

Scripture: Luke 4:1-13

THIS WEEK, CHOOSE to practice solitude thirty minutes daily, or for at least two hours in one day. This is not just a time to be alone but to be present to yourself without reading, music, or conversation. Toward the end of your time in solitude, journal about your experience—what you felt, heard, understood, how Jesus was present, and perhaps how he answered your question(s). Receive these words of guidance for your practice of solitude:

- While in solitude, ask Jesus this question: "Lord, what do you want to free me of?" and keep returning to this question when you feel your mind wander.
- You may feel anxious; you may think of a million things to do that would be a "better" use of your time. You may even feel guilty for "doing nothing." Don't take the bait. If the practice is challenging, you're doing it right.
- Notice all that is in your mind and heart, but don't rush into action. Simply observe what's in you, and listen to what Jesus wants to say to you about it. The things that come to mind may be some of what Jesus wants to provide freedom from!

Date(s) Used:_____

What did I learn about myself and/or God in this practice?

Second Sunday in Lent
Lament

Scripture: Luke 13:31-35

THIS WEEK, PRACTICE lament. Lament is uninhibited grief over what is not as it should be. As you go through your week, pay attention to what you see and hear in the news, in your own relationships, and on the street as you drive to work. Wherever there is injustice, brokenness, pain, suffering, or rejection, know that Jesus laments these things too. Ask Jesus to share his feelings with you as you join in his love for his people.

Date(s) Used: _____

What did I learn about myself and/or God in this practice?

_____
_____
_____
_____
_____
_____
_____

Third Sunday in Lent
Practice the Presence of God

Scripture: Luke 13:1-9

IN TELLING US about the fig tree, it seems Jesus is inviting us to consider that repentance may be more about recognizing that someone is doing something on our behalf than it is about what we are doing. This week, take on a practice of awareness by thinking of God as often as you can throughout the week so you can better recognize God's actions on your behalf. Many use a breath prayer to develop this habit, praying a simple sentence in rhythm with inhalation and exhalation. Observe what happens within your own spirit as your focus your attention on God's presence with you, and give thanks often. You can practice breath prayers as often as you think of it, using a phrase of your choice or one of these suggestions:

- Be still and know (*inhale*) that I am God (*exhale*).
- Jesus, free me (*inhale*) to hear and obey (*exhale*).

Date(s) Used: _____

What did I learn about myself and/or God in this practice?

Fourth Sunday in Lent
Praying Psalm 107

Scripture: Luke 15:1-3, 11b-32

THIS WEEK, PRAY with Psalm 107, allowing the ancient words to shape your conversation with God. The psalmist both celebrates God's ability to find, rescue, and save and also reminds God's people of the many ways they have needed to be found, rescued, and saved. Use these questions to help you pray along with the psalm:

- Which part of the psalm do you find the most relatable? Insert your own name among the words and make it a praise that is specific to you.
- Whom do you know wandering in wastelands (v. 4), sitting in deepest gloom (v. 10), suffering the pain of foolish decisions (v. 17), or in the middle of a storm (vv. 25–26)? Pray for them by name, asking that the Lord would do for them what the psalmist says he has done for others.
- What great desire or need feels entirely impossible to you? What injustice done to others weighs heavy upon you? Carry these concerns with you as you pray with verses 33–43.

After you have finished your time in prayer, take a moment for reflection. What was it like to remember your own experience? How is God inviting you to pray for others? Is there anything you are being asked or invited to do for any of those you prayed for?

Date(s) Used:_____

What did I learn about myself and/or God in this practice?

Fifth Sunday in Lent
Imaginative Prayer of Receiving the Sun

Scripture: John 12:1-8

JESUS WAS ABLE to give and receive love freely because he experienced God's love without any barriers in his own life. This week, we will practice an imaginative prayer adapted from Jesuit priest Joseph Tetlow so that we may receive and reflect God's love unhindered. Find a time when you can sit in the sunshine for at least thirty minutes. Imagine God as the sun and yourself as a mirror. Mirrors are not perfect; some lose silvering as they age, and others crack and chip. But all mirrors reflect light when they are pointed in the right direction. As you consider the condition and direction of your mirror, pray for the openness to receive all the love God wants to give, without any hindrances or barriers. After your time in prayer, you may want to journal your experience to recall it later.

Date(s) Used: _____

What did I learn about myself and/or God in this practice?

Palm Sunday/Sixth Sunday in Lent
Fasting

Scripture: Luke 19:28-40

FASTING IS SIMPLY the practice of saying no to something we usually say yes to, whether it's food, entertainment, or a certain kind of privilege. Each no is a small kind of death, and we are reminded all the more of Jesus's willing submission to death. We may also hear an invitation to die to something that is keeping us from hearing and responding to Jesus in obedience. Choose one of these suggestions to practice fasting this week:

- Fast meat, sugar, or another favorite food or drink all week.
- Fast one meal each day.
- Fast all food from sundown Friday to sundown Saturday.
- Fast from all entertainment, games, and/or social media.

Date(s) Used:_____

What did I learn about myself and/or God in this practice?

THE SEASON OF EASTER

On Easter Sunday we celebrate God's promise of resurrection coming to life in the resurrected Christ—the future reality rushing into our present moment. But Easter is not something we can encapsulate in a single day. It requires a fifty-day season to probe, ponder, and practice the deep and wonderful mystery of resurrection.

The ancients referred to Easter as the eighth day of creation because, on Easter, God began the work of making all things new, beginning with resurrecting Christ from the dead. In Easter we hear God proclaim, "I am making everything new!" (Revelation 21:5), and we affirm that, indeed, "the old has gone, the new is here!" (2 Corinthians 5:17).

When we observe Easter as a season, we have time to experience that resurrection is God's new creation made real not just in Jesus but also in all of us who are in Christ. There is plenty of time to marvel in this good news because we aren't forced to cram it all in on one day. We are given time to notice where new life is springing up around us and inside of us. Easter is the season of learning how to live a new kind of life, called resurrection. *May you experience the joy, the freedom, and the excitement of new life in these days.*

Easter Sunday
Cultivate Joy

Scripture: John 20:1-18

JOY IS A natural product of the resurrected life, but sometimes we need to *remember* the joy that is ours. This week, make intentional plans to spend at least two hours doing something that brings you joy. You may consider picking up an old favorite sport you haven't had time to play lately, pulling out your crafting box, playing catch at the park, or listening to your favorite music. Whatever you choose, allow it to lead you into joy and receive this gift as part of the resurrected life.

Date(s) Used: _____

What did I learn about myself and/or God in this practice?

Second Sunday of Easter
Listening to the Persecuted Church

Scripture: John 20:19-31

> *"We are pressed on every side by troubles, but we are not crushed. We are perplexed, but not driven to despair. We are hunted down, but never abandoned by God. We get knocked down, but we are not destroyed."*
>
> —2 Corinthians 4:8–9, NLT
> (words from a persecuted leader of the church)

THOSE WHO FOLLOW the resurrected Christ follow the same rule he does: no locked door will keep him out. There are many Christians around the world who find locked doors on all sides, but that doesn't stop them. While we mourn the hardships endured by brothers and sisters in areas of the world that are hostile to the gospel, we have much to learn from their emboldened, persistent witness. This week, spend time reading stories of these men and women through Voice of the Martyrs (www.voiceofthemartyrs.com). Invite the Holy Spirit to use their lives to teach and challenge you as you listen to them and pray for them. Pray that the resurrecting power of the gospel will not be stopped.

Date(s) Used: _____

What did I learn about myself and/or God in this practice?

Third Sunday of Easter
Write Words of Encouragement

Scripture: John 21:1-19

FEEDING SHEEP IS not an especially complicated or glorious task, nor is it something only wealthy or highly educated people can do. Each of us who has been nurtured by Jesus has the capacity to nurture others around us. This week, join in the task of caring for Jesus's flock by writing a supportive letter to a person who may need a word of encouragement. If you can't think of anyone, ask the Lord to give you a name and to give you a sense of what that person needs to hear. Your note doesn't have to be long, fancy, or profound. Sometimes just knowing we are thought of is encouragement enough.

Date(s) Used:_____

What did I learn about myself and/or God in this practice?

_____
_____
_____
_____
_____

Fourth Sunday of Easter
Listening

Scripture: John 10:22-30

ALL TOO OFTEN we practice one-sided conversations with God while we do all the talking. This week, practice *listening* for the voice of God. If you have a regular prayer time, include two minutes of silence in which you listen for God. If you don't have a regular prayer time, choose and protect a time of day when you can spend at least two minutes listening for God. Begin your time of listening with a simple prayer such as, *"I am listening, Lord. What do you want to say to me?"* Do not be discouraged if you do not hear something right away! Continue this practice throughout the week, and remember that you are *practicing*, not performing.

Date(s) Used: _____

What did I learn about myself and/or God in this practice?

Fifth Sunday of Easter
Hospitality

Scripture: Acts 11:1-18

PETER WAS QUESTIONED by the Jerusalem leaders because he spent time where they thought he shouldn't—in the home of a gentile (see Acts 10). What they didn't understand was that the gospel was—and is!—for all people. This week, practice the fullness of gospel hospitality by creating space for others in your life. It may feel more comfortable to extend hospitality to those who are like us, but we don't need the Spirit of God in order to do that. Ask and allow the Spirit to lead you where you wouldn't go on your own. To practice this radically hospitable gospel way of life, go out of your way to spend time with someone you normally wouldn't spend time with. Go to coffee or lunch with a coworker of a different ethnicity, invite a neighbor of a different religion over to dinner, or spend time with someone who has decidedly different political views than you.

Date(s) Used: _____

What did I learn about myself and/or God in this practice?

Sixth Sunday of Easter
Pray for the Seekers

Scripture: Acts 16:9-15

WHOM DO YOU know who is like Lydia—open, desiring, and seeking spiritual truth? They may practice their spirituality in ways that are foreign to you, but ask God to help you see past whether they are doing it "rightly" or "wrongly." Instead, ask to see the seekers in your life as God sees them: as people who are hungry, thirsty, and looking for truth. Pray earnestly for them by name this week, asking that, like Lydia, the full truth of the gospel would be revealed to them. Don't take it upon yourself to do more than pray, but be open if the Spirit asks you to be a messenger of the gospel as Paul was.

Date(s) Used: _____

What did I learn about myself and/or God in this practice?

HOLY DAYS: ASCENSION, PENTECOST, TRINITY SUNDAY

On Pentecost Sunday, we love to tell and retell the story of the Holy Spirit coming to the disciples in the upper room. Ascension Sunday and Trinity Sunday, on the other hand, are lesser known and, frankly, just not as exciting. But the observance of each day shapes us further into the way of Jesus as we encounter mystery, power, and a reality beyond our comprehension or control.

Ascension Sunday is the final Sunday in the season of Easter, and it marks the day that Christ ascended into heaven. We are reminded that Jesus did not remain on earth to continue a limited human existence in one place at one time. Rather, he ascended into the heavenly realm, where his presence and authority extend throughout all time and space. Observing this day gives us opportunity to consider this mystery, even if it doesn't offer many answers.

After Jesus's ascension, he gave the disciples a command to pray and wait for the Holy Spirit, who would act as an advocate, teacher, and comforter. On Pentecost Sunday, we remember when the Holy Spirit did indeed come as an unexpected mighty wind and fire—tangible evidence of God's presence from Israel's earliest days. This event is what we celebrate as the birthday of the church, when the disciples were empowered to preach in all kinds of languages and thousands believed the gospel of Jesus Christ.

On Trinity Sunday, we explore yet another mystery that will carry us through the rest of the year. There is no one scripture that specifically teaches us the doctrine of the Trinity. But early in the church's existence, as they

ruminated on Jesus's teachings and their own experiences, Christians began to recognize the three persons of God as Father, Son, and Spirit.

During these weeks of pondering mystery and power, our practices help us remember that we are only recipients of God's miraculous works. *May we receive, and may we respond in obedience.*

Ascension Sunday/ Seventh Sunday of Easter
Asking the Right Questions

Scripture: Acts 1:1–11

EVEN AFTER JESUS'S death and resurrection, the disciples still waited for their expectations of a political messiah to be fulfilled. After all they had seen and heard, they were still asking the wrong questions. Whenever we are solely focused on our desire of how things should go, we are guilty of the very same thing. This week, notice the questions you ask about yourself, about your world, and about God. There aren't necessarily any bad questions; but there are many that will go unanswered simply because we're asking the wrong ones. So here are some questions you can ask of God this week:

- Am I asking the right questions?
- Can you point me in the right direction so I can see what you are doing?
- What do *you* want me to be curious about, or ask for?

Date(s) Used:_____

What did I learn about myself and/or God in this practice?

Pentecost Sunday
Cross-Cultural Experience

Scripture: Acts 2:1-21

THE GLORY OF God shines in the diversity of his people, and God delights in bringing them together. This week, participate in the Spirit's unifying work by going somewhere you don't belong. Shop at a grocery store that specializes in food from an international culture. Worship with a congregation where the majority of people don't have your skin color or language. Eat at a restaurant where the menu isn't in English. While in this non-belonging space, notice what makes you feel uncomfortable and what makes you feel welcome. Be an observer of the differences, but work hard not to judge whether something is better or worse than what you're used to. Ask the Spirit to help you see God at work in unfamiliar places with language you don't understand. Pray also that you will be able to provide hospitality and compassion to those who feel they don't belong in the places you normally go.

Date(s) Used: _____

What did I learn about myself and/or God in this practice?

Trinity Sunday
Discernment

Scripture: John 16:12-15

WE RECEIVE AN abundance of words every day, and they all claim to be true. In fact, many may even use Scripture to prove their veracity. So how do we know what messages are the *truth* spoken by the Spirit? It requires the often underdeveloped spiritual muscle of discernment: a careful and constant examination of the messages we hear and the inner motivations we feel. The Spirit repeats what Jesus has said, points us toward God, and guides us into deeper relationship with God. So we can discern the Spirit's activity by looking toward Jesus, and also by looking within, at what's happening in our own spirit. This week, carefully examine the messages you receive, both from within yourself and from all the external voices in your life. Ask these questions as you listen for the sound of the Spirit's voice:

- Is this consistent with Jesus's own words and actions?
- Does this draw me closer to God or make me want to move further from God?
- What does this produce in my own spirit? Am I moving toward love, joy, hope, and peace? Or am I moving toward contempt, discontent, and anxiety?

Date(s) Used:_____

What did I learn about myself and/or God in this practice?

ORDINARY TIME

It seems significant that Trinity Sunday is our entryway into the longest "non-season season" of the Christian calendar: Ordinary Time. Like the doctrine of the Trinity, which the church discovered through the ordinary ebbs and flows of life, so in Ordinary Time we learn to walk with Jesus in the days that go unmarked and unnamed.

The seasons of Advent, Christmas, Epiphany, Lent, and Easter heighten our awareness for what God is doing in the world, but the months in Ordinary Time can have a way of dulling our awareness. The summer and back-to-school months also bring disruptions to our schedules with travel and vacations, followed by a flurry of activity to get back into gear. If we are not careful, we can check out altogether until, suddenly, it's time for Advent again!

If we learn to pay attention, however, we will find that some of the most ordinary things are actually extraordinary things that we just get used to—because they happen all the time. The days grow longer and then shorter again as evidences of our planet's movement around the sun. Seeds—once just tiny bits buried in soil—grow into beautiful flowers, sweet fruit, and nourishing vegetables. Our playgrounds echo with the sounds of shrieks and laughter. Bike paths and lakes and sidewalks fill with people enjoying God's good creation. The wonders of Ordinary Time are all around us.

And in these wonders of Ordinary Time, we are invited into a new experience of our triune God at work. While the seasons invite us to walk through the story of Jesus, we now have opportunity to notice how Jesus is walking with us. We find freedom to explore the particular themes of our own journey as we discern the Spirit's guidance in the very ordinary activities of life.

The Lectionary offers scheduled texts for each Sunday in Ordinary Time, but the Ordinary Time practices in this book are organized by theme rather than scriptural text. Using the freedom and discernment of Ordinary Time, you can hop and skip around, choosing a pattern of practices that best fits your own journey through these weeks. Directly following the Ordinary Time section is one that contains practices designed for specific events that may occur during our observance of Ordinary Time, or at any other time throughout the year. These events and the practices for them include election day, vacation, and tragedy.

The practices of Ordinary Time are designed to help us partner with the Spirit in growing good fruit in ourselves. *May you be aware of God in all the ordinary places, and may you know comfort and peace as Jesus walks with you there.*

PRACTICING THE LORD'S PRAYER

The prayer Jesus teaches us to pray is our entrance into living in relationship with God. The following eight practices invite us not only to say Jesus's prayer but also to take it on as a way of life.

Practicing the Lord's Prayer
Desiring our Father

"Our Father in heaven,"
—Matthew 6:9b, NLT

THIS WEEK, USE this prayer of Father Henri Nouwen (1932–1996) as you seek our Father in heaven.

O Lord, who else or what else can I desire but you? You are my Lord, Lord of my heart, mind, and soul. You know me through and through. In and through you everything that is finds its origin and goal. You embrace all that exists and care for it with divine love and compassion.

Why, then, do I keep expecting happiness and satisfaction outside of you? Why do I keep relating to you as one of my many relationships, instead of my only relationship, in which all other ones are grounded? Why do I keep looking for popularity, respect from others, success, acclaim, and sensual pleasures? Why, Lord, is it so hard for me to make you the only one? Why do I keep hesitating to surrender myself totally to you?

Let me be reborn in you and see through you the world in the right way, so that all my actions, words, and thoughts can become a hymn of praise to you.

Date(s) Used: _____

What did I learn about myself and/or God in this practice?

_____
_____
_____
_____
_____

Ordinary Time

Practicing The Lord's Prayer
Margin

"May your name be kept holy."
—Matthew 6:9c, NLT

IN HIS BOOK *Good and Beautiful God*, James Bryan Smith argues that living with healthy margins is essential to a holy life. Many of us suffer from isolation, hurry, and tiredness, which are not holy at all. Jesus invites us into a way of holiness that is wholeness: rest for our bodies and restoration for our souls. This week, practice margin by creating empty space in each day of the week. If that seems impossible, consider some of these options:

- Plan to arrive at appointments ten minutes early rather than getting there exactly on time (or late).
- Cut out unnecessary entertainment activities.
- When creating your schedule, consider whether each activity is essential for your work or your family. Commit only to what is essential.

Date(s) Used:_____

What did I learn about myself and/or God in this practice?

Practicing The Lord's Prayer
Play

> *"May your kingdom come soon."*
> —Matthew 6:10a, NLT

WE MIGHT THINK that the kingdom of God comes by buckling down and working really hard. But Jesus talks about the kingdom as a joyful surprise, even a party. When we play, we live into the truth that God's kingdom is a gift that brings us rest and joy, and frees us to share it with others. This week, make intentional plans to spend time playing. Play is something that doesn't always feel productive, and it's often something that makes you lose track of time. If you have a hard time remembering how to play, spend some time with young children and just join them in what they do so naturally.

Date(s) Used:_____

What did I learn about myself and/or God in this practice?

Ordinary Time

Practicing The Lord's Prayer
Wants Check

"May your will be done on earth, as it is in heaven."
—Matthew 6:10b, NLT

IN TWENTY-FIRST-CENTURY AMERICA, the concept of getting what *I* want has become the highest priority and the ultimate good. It is highly unusual, and rather uncomfortable, to ask that God gets everything God wants, instead of asking that we get everything we want! This week, take at least thirty minutes and make a list of everything you want—both material and immaterial. When the list is complete, pray over it, asking if any of those things show up on the list God wants for you. Pray that the Spirit would help you desire what *God* wants, and ask what to do about the list of things that only *you* want.

Date(s) Used: _____

What did I learn about myself and/or God in this practice?

_____
_____
_____
_____
_____

YEAR C

Practicing The Lord's Prayer
Giving Daily Bread

"Give us today the food we need,"
—Matthew 6:11, NLT

IT IS STRIKING that we are invited to pray for our bread. Within this collective request, there is room to pray alongside those who do not have food in their cupboards, money to buy it, or even a kitchen to cook it. If you already have enough daily bread for yourself (think: food, clothing, shelter, and other basic resources), ask the Lord to guide you this week so you can be a means of answering someone else's prayer for daily bread. You might volunteer or donate to a food pantry, buy a hungry person food, or give away what you don't need.

Date(s) Used: _____

What did I learn about myself and/or God in this practice?

_____
_____
_____
_____
_____

Ordinary Time

Practicing The Lord's Prayer
Contemplating Forgiveness

"And forgive us our sins, as we have forgiven those who sin against us."
—Matthew 6:12, NLT

CONTEMPLATION, OR IMAGINATIVE prayer, allows us to engage in conversation with Jesus as we imagine ourselves in the words of Scripture. This week, contemplate a story Jesus told about forgiveness. Set aside at least thirty minutes for this practice as you follow the pattern below. When you are finished, write down any insights you gained.

- Begin by asking the Holy Spirit to lead you through this practice.
- Read Matthew 18:21–33 slowly at least two times.
- Imagine the scene and characters of the story as if you were there yourself. Take time to enter into the emotions of the servant whose debt was forgiven:
  - What experience of forgiveness has given you freedom?
  - What thoughts, emotions, or questions rise up in you?
  - Who is indebted to you, and how do you feel toward that person?
- After you have personally identified with the truth of the story, imagine yourself next to Jesus, and talk to him about what you have experienced.
- Ask Jesus to help you know the fullness of forgiveness you have received, and to whom you need to extend forgiveness.

Date(s) Used: _____

What did I learn about myself and/or God in this practice?

Practicing The Lord's Prayer
Going on a God Hunt

"And don't let us yield to temptation, but rescue us from the evil one."
—Matthew 6:13, NLT

LIVING THE WAY of Jesus means that we not only walk *with* Jesus but also that we *follow* him. He has already gone into the darkest, most evil places we can imagine, and he is working even there to bring deliverance. We do not confront the darkness of evil with only our small candle to light the way; rather, we follow the light of Jesus that is already present. This week, cultivate an awareness of God by intentionally looking for signs of God everywhere—in every person, circumstance, news story, and activity. When you encounter evil and fear, pray the Lord's Prayer (especially the part asking God to deliver us from evil), and ask God to show you where he is already present in that situation.

Date(s) Used: _____

What did I learn about myself and/or God in this practice?

Ordinary Time

Practicing The Lord's Prayer
Gratitude

IN EXPRESSING GRATITUDE, we remember that we are recipients of good that we ourselves have not produced. God's power, glory, and the goodness of his kingdom are all around us! This week, keep a list of all the good you encounter, pausing to write it down and express gratitude. Be reminded that God's kingdom is larger, better, and more beautiful than we can comprehend.

Date(s) Used: _____

What did I learn about myself and/or God in this practice?

NURTURING THE FRUIT OF THE SPIRIT

It is the Spirit's work to grow good fruit in us, but we can engage in practices that either encourage or hinder that work. Use the next eighteen practices to partner with God as the Spirit grows good, beautiful fruit in you.

Love, Joy, and Peace
Sabbath

SABBATH IS THE gift of the Good Shepherd, who restores our souls: a twenty-four-hour break from all work. This week, plan how you will practice Sabbath. If you are concerned you can't do a full twenty-four hours, commit to at least twelve hours. Remember that Sabbath is not a reward for getting everything done; it is a break from doing the things that need to get done. If it bothers you to leave things undone while you practice Sabbath, know that this too is an opportunity to grow in grace. Think through these questions to help you determine what you will and won't do on your Sabbath day:

- What activities help me remember my true identity in God, and what activities pull me away from that understanding?
- What activities bring me great peace and joy, and which ones make me feel heavy?
- Which relationships nurture my God desires, and how I can give more time to them?
- How can I grow in gratitude for what I already have?

Date(s) Used: _____

What did I learn about myself and/or God in this practice?

Love, Joy, and Peace
Celebrate a Saint

THERE ARE MANY who have gone before us who can serve as mentors for us as we walk the way of Jesus. This week, think of someone who has modeled for you what it means to be a saint: a person devoted to God and taken over by love. Write a brief note of celebration and gratitude for their presence in your life. If they are no longer living, express your gratitude to God, and find someone who knew this person to share it with.

Date(s) Used: _____

What did I learn about myself and/or God in this practice?

_____
_____
_____
_____
_____

Love, Joy, and Peace
Generosity

WE ARE SURROUNDED by and inundated with a myth of scarcity, or the idea that we must protect what we have because there is not enough to go around. As people living in God's kingdom, though, we are ruled not by scarcity but by *abundance*. God has more than enough, and he shares it freely and with joy. Everything we have has been given to us. It is all "manna," given to us daily by our more-than-generous God. God's provision makes it possible for us to be generous as well, no matter how much we have. This week, practice generosity as you buy someone's coffee, give to a ministry, or get a grocery gift card for a neighbor who needs it. Oddly enough, the more we practice generosity, the more joyful we become.

Date(s) Used: _____

What did I learn about myself and/or God in this practice?

Love, Joy, and Peace
Breath Prayer

OUR BREATH IS not something we think about often, but it is our constant source of life. The practice of breath prayer (or centering prayer) reminds us that God's presence is as close and as real as our breath, and just as necessary for our lives. This week, practice breath prayer as often as you think of it, but especially in times of worry or anxiety. Whenever you notice your breath getting faster, take it as a cue to focus on your breathing and on God's presence with you. Try one of these as breath prayers, or come up with one of your own:

- Be still and know (*inhale*) that I am God (*exhale*).
- I am deeply loved (*inhale*), and Christ dwells in me (*exhale*).
- The joy of the Lord (*inhale*) is my strength (*exhale*).

Date(s) Used:_____

What did I learn about myself and/or God in this practice?

Love, Joy, and Peace
Think about Better Things

"Since you have been raised to new life with Christ, set your sights on the realities of heaven, where Christ sits in the place of honor at God's right hand. Think about the things of heaven, not the things of earth."

—Colossians 3:1–2, NLT

THIS WEEK, PRACTICE pulling your thoughts to what is better. Any time you find yourself concerned with an issue, good or bad, use it as a cue to think on the astounding gift of being raised to new life with Christ. To help you in this practice, you might want to write these words from Colossians 3 somewhere you will see often.

Date(s) Used: _____

What did I learn about myself and/or God in this practice?

Love, Joy, and Peace
Tell a God Story

WHEN HAVE YOU experienced a God story? Think about a time you experienced God's miraculous provision, received clear guidance, or witnessed his astonishing activity. Look for an opportunity to tell this story to someone this week. When we retell these experiences, we are reminded all over again of God's goodness. Our God stories bring us joy, nurture our trust, and encourage others. You will be surprised at what telling a story can do!

Date(s) Used:_____

What did I learn about myself and/or God in this practice?

Patience, Kindness, and Goodness
Driving the Speed Limit

OBEDIENCE IS DIFFICULT for people of all ages because, if we're honest, we just don't want to submit to another person or authority. Submission doesn't mean we don't think for ourselves or lose our autonomy, but it does mean we suppress our own desire for control. This week, take simple steps of obedience by following the speed limit every time you drive. If you don't drive, take care to follow all posted signs for pedestrians and/or cyclists. When you find yourself speeding or jaywalking, let it serve as a reminder of your own difficulty with submission, and your impatience. Ask the Spirit to give you a desire to want God's authority in your life and to grow in you the fruit of patience.

Date(s) Used:_____

What did I learn about myself and/or God in this practice?

Patience, Kindness, and Goodness
Write a Note

A HANDWRITTEN NOTE is a gift of time that few of us receive much in our age of emails and text messages. This week, carve out time to write and mail a short note to a friend or family member. It doesn't have to say profound or spiritual things, and it doesn't need to be long. It just needs to be in your handwriting—a simple gift of your time and thought. If you have trouble deciding whom to write or what to say, ask Jesus to suggest someone who might need it this week.

Date(s) Used: _____

What did I learn about myself and/or God in this practice?

Patience, Kindness, and Goodness
Eat Together

EVERY TIME WE receive Communion, we remember the life, death, and resurrection of Jesus that brings us into new life. But his presence with us is not limited to bread and wine; we are invited to remember him as often as we break bread together. This week, any time you are eating with your family or friends, look for God in your midst. If you do not usually eat with others, make a point to share a meal with at least one other person this week. Be reminded that Jesus ate normal meals with his friends and family too. Any moment can become a holy moment when we recognize the holy among us.

Date(s) Used: _____

What did I learn about myself and/or God in this practice?

Patience, Kindness, and Goodness
Three Blessings

THIS WEEK, LOOK for opportunities to extend kindness to others. With prayerful intention and planning, choose three actions that will bless someone else. You might write a note of encouragement, buy someone's lunch, give an unexpected gift, or simply show up and have conversation with a person who usually sits alone. If and when you are tempted to shrug off the work of blessing others, allow Christ's love and blessing to you fuel your desire to bless others.

Date(s) Used: _____

What did I learn about myself and/or God in this practice?

_____
_____
_____
_____
_____
_____

Patience, Kindness, and Goodness
Value Search

THROUGHOUT SCRIPTURE, GOD seems intent on using all the "wrong" people to accomplish his work: liars, swindlers, prostitutes, the uneducated, those with disabilities and flaws. Jesus put words to this odd value system when he said blessed are the poor, and the hungry and thirsty, and those who mourn. In the kingdom, there's a high value placed on knowing one's need. This week, take notice of what you value in the people you work with, in your family, and in yourself. Ask the Spirit to help you see what God values in you and in others around you. Be on the lookout for those who are peacemakers, those who are meek, and those who are gentle. They often are overlooked by the world's value system, but they are the highly valued and blessed citizens of God's kingdom.

Date(s) Used: _____

What did I learn about myself and/or God in this practice?

_____
_____
_____
_____
_____
_____

Ordinary Time

Patience, Kindness, and Goodness
Not Having to Be Right

OUR CULTURE PLACES a high value on being right, and we all go to great lengths to prove to others that we are right. This week, in an effort to remember that knowledge is not the greatest virtue in God's kingdom, practice giving up your need to be right. Unless doing so would cause harm to you or someone else, let the other person have the last word when you are contradicted. Whenever the issue at hand is none other than your own desire to be right, let the argument go. If a situation really does require that you bring correction, do so with gentleness, respect, and discretion.

Date(s) Used: _____

What did I learn about myself and/or God in this practice?

Faithfulness, Gentleness, and Self-Control
Tithing

THIS WEEK, TAKE on the practice of giving a tithe (ten percent) of your income to your local church. If this is a brand-new practice for you, it may seem impossible to start by giving a whole ten percent. It is important to start where you are able, instead of waiting to do it exactly the way you think it should be done. In this spirit, ask the Lord's guidance to determine what percentage to give—perhaps five percent or two percent to begin. If tithing is already your regular practice, you may find the Lord asking you to increase the percentage you give. Whatever the amount, commit that money *first*, and use what is left for the rest of your expenses for this pay period. Especially if this is a new practice for you, make it as tangible as possible: get out cash or write a check, put it in an envelope, and bring it to place in the offering next week. This may feel risky. As we practice tithing, we also ask and trust our generous Lord of abundance to provide for us in ways we haven't yet experienced. The apostle Paul encourages us: "And my God will meet all your needs according to the riches of his glory in Christ Jesus" (Philippians 4:19).

Date(s) Used: _____

What did I learn about myself and/or God in this practice?

Faithfulness, Gentleness, and Self-Control
Praying the Daily Examen

ST. IGNATIUS, A fifteenth-century priest and the founder of the Jesuits, taught the Daily Examen as a way of praying in order to recognize God's presence and activity in our lives. Over time this practice grows our awareness of God, and we recognize the gift of God's awesome, abiding faithfulness. The more we experience God's faithfulness to us, the more we grow in our desire and capacity to be faithful as well. To practice the Examen this week, set aside three to five minutes at the same time every day. It may be helpful to use a journal to jot down your observations as you pray.

1. Ask the Holy Spirit to help you see the last twenty-four hours as God sees them.
2. Focus on the day's gifts and give thanks for them.
3. What invitations or opportunities did God give you? Notice any moments of strong emotion as clues to God's activity and your response.
4. Ask the Spirit to guide you to one particular event or emotion of the day that is important, and pray repentance, gratitude, or a request/petition accordingly.
5. As you look toward the next day, ask specifically for what you need.

Date(s) Used: _____

What did I learn about myself and/or God in this practice?

Faithfulness, Gentleness, and Self-Control
Daily Silence

WHEN THERE IS constant noise available all around us, choosing silence is an act of self-control, and it is also a practice that helps us grow in gentleness. To practice silence, choose a time of day that will be free of interruptions, perhaps first thing in the morning. Set an alarm or timer so you do not have to watch the time. Sit in the silence for five full minutes, without reading, writing, or listening to anything. Do not be alarmed if your mind jumps around to a million different things during this time. Be persistent in putting these things to rest, making space for God to speak into your stillness. Be reminded of God's presence, and ask for even greater awareness of the Spirit's work within you.

Date(s) Used:_____

What did I learn about myself and/or God in this practice?

Faithfulness, Gentleness, and Self-Control
Allow Interruptions

MOST OF OUR time is filled to capacity—people to see, things to do, places to go. Unexpected conversations and requests can become aggravating interruptions to a carefully planned day. This week, take on a practice of *allowing* interruptions as opportunities to participate in something greater than your own agenda. Open yourself to the kid who wants to have a conversation at the wrong time; the lonely person who talks to you in the grocery store; the phone call you know will take longer than you really want to give; the person who needs help even when you're in a hurry. As you practice interruption this week, remember the way Jesus allowed the voices on the margins to interrupt his life. Ask for the grace to see others as he does and to be moved by them as he is.

Date(s) Used:_____

What did I learn about myself and/or God in this practice?

Faithfulness, Gentleness, and Self-Control
Praying the Hours

IN HER BOOK *Saint Benedict on the Freeway*, Corinne Ware suggests that we reimagine the monastic practice of the hours to participate in God's work through our work. In the midst of all the regular and tedious work of life, monks made space to recognize that all time and activity was sacred because God was present. Traditionally there are eight times a day to observe the hours; this week, practice observing four. Set an alarm on your phone, watch, or computer to help you pause at these intervals in each day, and pray along the lines suggested below.

> *Lauds:* 6am/waking up: Welcome the light of a new day by giving thanks, reading Scripture, praying a familiar prayer, or just sitting with God in a few moments of silence.
>
> *Sext:* 12pm/midday: Pause for as long as you have to lift up concerns: coworkers, events you've heard on the news, a current work dilemma.
>
> *None:* 4pm/late afternoon: Reflect on the day, flushing out worry and regret, remembering moments of joy, choosing to forgive, or asking for forgiveness.
>
> *Vespers:* 9pm/end of day: The bookend to *lauds*, end the day with Scripture reading, prayer, or a word of blessing spoken over your loved ones.

Date(s) Used: _____

What did I learn about myself and/or God in this practice?

_____
_____
_____
_____
_____
_____

Faithfulness, Gentleness, and Self-Control
The Suscipe Prayer of St. Ignatius

THE FIRST WORD of this prayer, *suscipe*, is Latin for "take" or "receive." These words of St. Ignatius, founder of the Jesuits, have guided numerous Christ followers in joyful generosity for more than five hundred years. This week, use this prayer as your mealtime prayer as often as you eat:

Take, Lord, and receive all my liberty,
my memory, my understanding, and my entire will,
all I have and call my own.
You have given all to me.
To you, Lord, I return it.
Everything is yours; do with it what you will.
Give me only your love and your grace—that is enough for me.

Date(s) Used:_____

What did I learn about myself and/or God in this practice?

_____

_____

_____

_____

_____

_____

PRACTICES FOR NOT-SO-ORDINARY TIME: VACATION, ELECTIONS, TRAGEDY

In the midst of Ordinary Time there are often weeks that feel anything but ordinary. Vacation is a planned escape from the ordinary, while tragic events come unexpectedly and uproot all sense of normalcy. And, for those who follow the news closely, election season often has a life all its own. Find these practices when you need them, and use them to connect you to the God who is unchanging but certainly not ordinary.

A Practice for Vacation
Awareness of God in Creation

AS OFTEN AS you are able this week, allow yourself time to become deeply absorbed in nature as a way of experiencing God's goodness. Instead of rushing past your ordinary landscape, take some time to notice the extraordinary in it. Pay great attention to the sights, sounds, and colors of nature, and marvel in them. As you sit in creation, give your attention to *enjoying* it as you would a famous painting in an art museum. God—the Master Artist—has put all of creation before us to bring forth joy and beauty. Know that, even if it looks like you are doing nothing, you are engaged in holy work.

Date(s) Used: _____

What did I learn about myself and/or God in this practice?

A Practice for Election Season
Live Like Jesus Is Lord

THE KINGDOM OF God is everlasting and unshakable, regardless of the outcome of any election in any nation. Throughout history, some governments have made it more difficult to live the way of Jesus and some easier. But Christians in all nations live the way of Jesus no matter who holds earthly power. This week, remind yourself often that Jesus is your Lord and that your allegiance is to him alone. If you find yourself getting upset about national politics or conversations with others, look to Jesus for guidance. What does Jesus think about this situation? What does Jesus invite you to do in the midst of it?

Date(s) Used:_____

What did I learn about myself and/or God in this practice?

A Practice during Tragedy
Pondering

IN HIS BOOK *Sacred Fire*, Ronald Rolheiser describes the Hebrew notion of pondering as an action that holds and carries tension in order to transform it. This practice of pondering keeps us from conducting the forces of hatred and violence, even if it means we absorb them in ourselves. Rolheiser asserts that one of the clearest pictures of this practice is gentle, loving, faithful Mary at the foot of the cross. There are times when we are called to fight injustice with everything we have. But there are other times in which we are invited to observe evil, ponder it, and allow the Spirit to transform the energy of hatred into something beautiful within us. When you encounter evil this week, in whatever form, consider this invitation. Ask the Spirit to guide you to know when you are invited to action and when you are invited to ponder.

Date(s) Used: _____

What did I learn about myself and/or God in this practice?

_____
_____
_____
_____
_____

CHRIST THE KING SUNDAY

Christ the King Sunday is the final Sunday of Ordinary Time, before the church year begins anew with Advent. Once again, we will grow in hopeful anticipation as we learn to wait in the dark. But if we're not careful, we could be fooled into thinking that all we have to hope for and expect is the presents, the decadent food, or the glittering decorations of our Christmas celebrations.

Christ the King Sunday offers us a clear picture of what we expectantly await during Advent—our King and his kingdom to come on earth, even as it is in heaven. We are reminded that our King is unlike any other king, and his kingdom unlike any other kingdom. So we should not be surprised if we find ourselves becoming unlike other people.

In this week before Advent, we enter a kind of preparation before the preparation. *Let us fix our eyes on King Jesus, and may we find our home in his kingdom.*

Christ the King Sunday
Daily Reading of the Christ Hymn

Scripture: Luke 23:33-43

READ AND MEDITATE on the Christ Hymn (Colossians 1:15–20) every day this week. After you have read it, spend at least five minutes just thinking about it. Allow your mind to wander around the words and ideas expressed in this ancient poem, and resist the urge to "figure it out." Notice what insights and emotions emerge as you spend time contemplating King Jesus, writing down anything you want to remember.

Date(s) Used: _____

What did I learn about myself and/or God in this practice?

_____
_____
_____
_____
_____